KEEPING LOVE Alive

TOOLS THAT WORK FOR COUPLES

MONA COATES, Ph.D.

THERAPY OPTIONS PRESS
Santa Monica • California

Cover & book design by Tania Baban-Natal,
    Conflux Press www.confluxpress.com

Cover photo of Mona Coates by Colleen Bevacqua

ISBN: 978-0-9835562-2-0

First published in 2018

Printed in the United States of America

THERAPY OPTIONS PRESS
855 10th Street #208
Santa Monica, California
310-393-5372
www.judithsearle.com

For Eddie — the love of my life

TABLE OF CONTENTS

ACKNOWLEDGMENTS   7

INTRODUCTION   11

PART I
WHY RELATIONSHIPS SUCCEED
    AND FAIL   21

PART II
THE TEN TOOLS:

1 UNDERPINNINGS:
Six Qualities to Help Love Thrive   59

2 LOVE, LIKING AND LUST:
What Shape Is Your Triangle?   81

3 LOVE STYLES:
Different Ways of Giving Love   97

4 INTIMACY RATING:
How Do You Score?   111

5 BATTLE BETWEEN THE SEXES:
Guidelines for Getting It   131

6 GETTING TO KNOW YOU:
Sentence Completion   141

7 SUBTYPES:
The Hidden Level of Personality   153

8 COMPATIBILITY RATING:
How Compatible Are You?   165

9 RESOLVING CONFLICT:
Turning Right   183

10 ATTITUDE AND MINDSET:
Finding a Different Street   195

PART III
IF YOU NEED FURTHER HELP   207

ABOUT THE AUTHOR   219

ACKNOWLEDGMENTS

This is the second book I've written with Judith Searle as my editor, co-producer, and primary source of inspiration. Her enthusiasm and dedication to this work have been profound.

This book would not exist without her steadfast belief in me and my work.

It is extremely rare in one's personal and/or professional life to have found a "working" partner with whom one is exceptionally compatible—matching one's own level of intensity, interest and commitment.

In fact, this second book was originally suggested by Judith as an outgrowth of our first book, *Sex, Love and Your Personality*. What a "gift " it has been to navigate through another book with someone so dedicated and seasoned as a writer, editor and producer. It has been my honor and privilege to again work with Judith.

As always, my dear husband, Eddie Jacobs has been my main source of emotional support from the beginning. During much of my 38 years of college teaching and now my 41 years as a psychotherapist (primarily marriage counseling and sex therapy), his computer skills and technical abilities have always been crucial in the production of each Tool—in a readable, inviting and professionally impeccable format. I was fortunate through the years to have written many articles, exercises and Tools (a few of which are included in this book) that he painstakingly formatted and elegantly produced as handouts for my thousands of students and therapy clients. It is on his shoulders that I stand for the original and professional production of my numerous surveys, articles, exercises and handwritten Tools.

His steadfast love and encouragement have been the main rock of support in all of my ventures.

In so many ways, I am especially indebted to and grateful for Tania Baban-Natal—the very talented artist, designer and formatter of this book. Likewise, I am deeply appreciative of the assistance of Jim Natal; his strength, efficiency, solid advice and professional suggestions for publication have been invaluable.

As always, my deepest appreciation and admiration go to my clients (over a period of four decades) who have trusted me, risked becoming vulnerable and worked hard to resolve their therapeutic issues, marital conflicts and communication problems. Staying "in the trenches" with them, step by step, has been my ultimate privilege and source of gratification.

I an grateful for their trust in me professionally and ultimately for their decision to open their hearts and minds to allow more love "in" and help it grow and thrive.

For the many writers and therapists that have come before me, I am eternally grateful. Their professional work and insights have paved the way for better techniques and Tools to be used in psychotherapy.

I've quoted a few of them in this book—Simon Baron-Cohen, Gary Chapman, John Grey and Harville Hendrix—and many others have supplied much of the background knowledge on which this book was built.

There now exist thousands of other researchers, therapists and authors who have helped produce the body of knowledge that we so casually refer to as "psychology." To each of them I owe special appreciation for their professional insights.

— Mona Coates, Ph.D.

INTRODUCTION

Most of us, most of the time, want to love and be loved. And we're hopeful that this love will grow and thrive. That's the goal.

So how is it, then, that love relationships can get so complicated? So twisted? So painful and distorted? So unhappy and unsatisfying?

These shifts happen because we want to protect ourselves, to defend ourselves from our fears and anxieties. We try to avoid the pain and suffering inherent in the process of loving and wanting to be loved by another person.

Our fears lead us to try to control our mate, using manipulation, threats, enticements and seduction to insure their compliance. We mistakenly feel this will banish our suffering and fear.

Or we may pretend we are indifferent, "go numb," become passive, avoid showing that we care, thinking this will "wake them up," so that our own anxieties will be assuaged.

We might even martyr ourselves, playing the victim—the one who has been cheated out of equal consideration. In this scenario, we foolishly hope that our martyrdom will cause our partner to appreciate all we've done—to "sit up and take notice."

Such tactics rarely work over the long term. That's because

our hearts aren't open and truly loving. Our minds and attitudes are basically rigid and closed, our opinions and prejudices solid and unwavering, so that new information, new ideas and potential changes of habit cannot penetrate this fortress we have built around our own minds.

Most couples *think* they know far more about their partner than they actually do. Our own personality biases, fears and defenses keep us well shielded from the truth. In order to avoid the pain, discomfort or embarrassment of actually learning something new about our relationship (or our self) we reinforce our defense mechanisms so we can continue seeing things the way we always have.

This way real love and growth get blocked off; our defensive posture prevents love from thriving. The great psychologist Carl Jung put it this way: "Neurosis is always a substitute for legitimate suffering."

As a young therapist I didn't understand the acuteness of his insight. But now, after forty years of experience in the trenches with clients, I'm familiar with the ways individuals and couples, seeking to avoid or deny their discomfort and suffering, have actually created more pain for themselves and curtailed the potential growth and evolution of their marriage. Such attitudes and defenses often result in even deeper problems.

At the same time, reflecting back over decades of clinical practice with all kinds of clients, I'm aware that many of them had a good foundation. Many couples had a shared culture, common values, goals and good reasons for wanting their marriage to thrive and their love to grow.

Most of the couples simply needed a little help—a boost and some direction as to how they might better handle the everyday differences, hurt feelings and arguments that arose; it's often these *minor problems* that get in the way of deeper intimacy.

Most of us sincerely want our marriage (or significant relationship) to grow, mature and thrive. This process is what brings us the joy and fulfillment we long for.

It is for this audience that I've written this book—to share the Tools and methods that over many years have proven to be of significant help.

• The Will to Utilize the Tools •

Even among the healthiest and happiest of couples, there are times when both partners suffer from common emotional dilemmas and a diminished ability to communicate.

Even highly functional couples occasionally find themselves caught in the crossfire of serious misunderstandings. Sometimes they simply lack the structure and methods (i.e., the Tools) to resolve their differences.

In many of these good relationships, there doesn't seem to be any real need for professional therapy. Yet some Tools might be quite helpful in their quest to deepen their understanding of one another. It's my hope that this book can be of significant assistance to those fundamentally healthy couples.

• Other Applications •

Another audience for whom this book is appropriate is those individuals and couples who are curious and adventurous, seekers after knowledge and experience. Some of them may be exploring the world of dating in search of a potential life partner. Several of these Tools could be extremely helpful in this context.

Other readers may simply be curious about what a "committed" relationship might involve. Or they may need some Tools to help them eliminate potential mates at an early stage, avoiding unproductive investments of time and energy.

Still other individuals are devoted to objective research, strongly motivated to know exactly how a "potential mate" might respond to some of the Tools described in this book.

Whether you're currently in a committed relationship or testing the waters for a possible mate, it might be worth your time to consider how the Tools I've described here might be useful in your quest for a deep connection with the right person.

In none of these instances would professional counseling be a necessity. Yet the effective use of some of these Tools might help prevent a marriage that never should have been, by disclosing at an early stage of relationship some "non-negotiable" differences or incompatibilities that would disqualify a potential mate.

For the most part, however, any couple's sincere desire to enrich or clarify their love relationship can be served by the use of these Tools.

In the stressful world we all live in, many couples have inadvertently allowed the intimacy in their relationship to slip away, falter or fracture. Perhaps that once romantic bond has weakened over time, simply from the pressure of such day-to-day burdens as children, bills, dual careers and/or illnesses.

To make a start on reversing these deficits takes a certain amount of personal discipline and a bit of time set aside, in order to make effective use of the Tools described in Part II.

But be assured that it is possible for these exercises to produce a powerful sense of clarity—about the information (and determination) required to help your love grow and thrive.

• Sustaining the Discomfort •

Some of these Tools, more than others, can produce a certain amount of discomfort, punctuated by moments of real pain. However, it is through these processes that honest feedback, genuine caring and empathy can emerge.

There is no great complexity—no high learning curve—involved in working with any of the Tools, which are self-explanatory. But it does take the will and the personal discipline to walk through any discomfort, awkwardness or fear that might arise.

The results of persisting through these rough places can be so rewarding, so informative, so empowering that achieving these breakthroughs is well worth the journey.

There is even greater satisfaction when certain behaviors are modified, changes are made, and attitudes are adjusted as a result of using the Tools.

Of course not all couples or individuals will be significantly helped or inspired by these methods. In many cases, it's possible that only one or two of the Tools will feel relevant or ultimately meaningful. In other cases, some couples have benefited enormously from most of the exercises presented. Much of the benefit depends upon the motivation and desire of the two people involved.

The real adventure of discovering deeper levels of your partner's feelings, attitudes and preferences can be highly informative and satisfying—even if you've been married for fifty years.

Most of us believe we know so much more about our mate's

needs, motives, desires and fears than is actually the case. Discovering deeper layers of your partner's inner psyche (as well as your own) can be an incredible adventure. It's worth your effort.

• Getting Started •

Without recourse to actual therapy sessions, it's up to you (the couple) to take the initiative and venture into choosing one or more of the Tools to get started.

In order to simplify couples' comparisons of and discussions about their written answers in some exercises, I've included duplicate pages of these exercises for certain Tools where appropriate. This is truly a Workbook in which you keep track of your own responses. Treat it like a journal.

Each of the Tools has been developed to provide a different pathway, process or exercise to assist readers on the journey toward clarifying or improving their love relationship.

Specifically, these Tools are intended for you to try, test, throw out or contemplate for your own unique circumstances.

I trust that even an honest discussion with your partner about the Tools can produce greater understanding and insight. This is never a waste of time: It's your love, your relationship—your future together.

In general, this will be a revealing and exciting process of discovery for most couples (with little interludes of pain or discomfort here and there).

It has been my experience that one or more of the Tools might be sufficient to resolve many immediate and/or minor problems, with no formal therapy needed. It is my hope that most couples can benefit greatly from at least one or two of the Tools, as they jump around to various parts of this book.

All of the individuals and couples described in this book are actual cases—most of them from my clinical practice. Confidentiality is always a necessary part of any professional psychotherapy; hence the names of all clients were changed in order to preserve their anonymity. All the essential facts, in every case, remain unchanged.

Help the love you already have to thrive. It can grow—and blossom into an even greater love.

—Mona Coates, Ph.D.
Huntington Beach, CA

— PART I —

WHY RELATIONSHIPS SUCCEED AND FAIL

Most of us, almost always, want our primary love relationship to *work*. This includes everything from a peak experience of melting together as one to the daily tasks of cooperation, problem solving and agreement making. All these things are integral parts of a functioning relationship.

Over the past 40 years social scientists, therapists and psychologists have accumulated a considerable body of useful knowledge about love relationships—what helps them thrive and what undermines them.

In this first section I'll briefly summarize this body of knowledge and my own clinical observations of clients struggling to form lasting and rewarding partnerships. We'll look at two broad areas of relationship research:

A) **What it takes:**
    the essential components of a loving, supportive union. What determines whether a given relationship will continue to grow, producing increasing intimacy, trust and comfort for the partners.

B) **When it fails:**
    what factors predict when a relationship is likely to disintegrate. What qualities in a romantic partnership contribute to couples dissolving their connection and/or divorcing.

WHAT IT TAKES

What makes a love relationship thrive and mature may appear self-evident: caring, devotion, love, trust and good communication are generally part of the picture. Words like these are easy enough to list. But putting such qualities into practice may be far more difficult when we're feeling angry, discounted or defensive.

What matters is *not* that we experience these negative feelings from time to time. We all do. What *does matter* is how we handle these emotions. From my clinical experience, the following nine factors summarize the conditions and qualities that make a love relationship work:

1. Flexibility

An attitude of flexibility and non-defensiveness can generate and sustain great understanding and closeness in a love relationship. Even when you're sure your opinion or habitual way of dealing with an issue is "the only right way," it's helpful to consider the possibility that your partner may have a different and valuable perspective.

Your partner has every right to her/his own opinion, regardless of what you think. Even when you're utterly confident about the superiority of your own assessment, show your mate the respect of "active listening" to her/his viewpoint and trying to understand it.

This behavior on your part creates trust and good will. When patience and kindness dominate your attitude, your partner can relax and at least feel respected.

In their helpful little book on myths about love, *Happily Ever After*, Linda and Charlie Bloom sum up this principle as follows: "Freeing ourselves from the need to be right . . . is not so much about changing our behavior as changing our *perspective*."

This kind of change is really about becoming more open, vulnerable and approachable.

2. Forgivness

Ultimately, forgiveness is a spiritual act. It is letting go of the hurts, insults and transgressions that may have blocked the flow of love between you and your partner.

The process of forgiveness is also a self-serving act. It is a way of purifying yourself through cleansing your own emotional palate. Once you no longer have to drag this baggage of resentment around with you, you become emotionally free.

Some people assume forgiveness implies that your partner is "off the hook"— that you're justifying his/her offense. In fact, this issue is irrelevant to your loving and intelligent decision to cleanse yourself emotionally.

The act of forgiveness allows you to be free to be present with your partner and get back to focusing on the love and intimacy you share.

Forgiveness can often involve a "do over." This happens when both partners—in a calm state—agree to re-enact the situation that caused the original breach, playing out *different* choices, responses, or decisions. In some cases this can bring a sense of closure and satisfaction to resolving the issue—giving the forgiveness an even stronger underpinning. Many couples have benefitted enormously from the exciting process of enacting a "do over."

3. Self-Discipline

With self-discipline, a person remains focused on the underlying goals of the partnership/marriage, including the willingness to "keep on keeping on." This involves mustering the endurance and stamina to stop arguing and seek solutions to problems.

This may also mean taking a break at crucial moments in order to explore a different perspective. Julia Coldwell in her *Relationship Skills Workbook* offers this sensible advice for problem solving: "If you haven't resolved an issue in fifteen minutes, *stop talking*. Do something, anything else. Come back to the issue when. . . ."

Important issues are often solved easily when *both* partners have moved past their defensiveness into a calmer space. Once both of you can commit to following some basic rules for self-disclosure and effective listening, many issues are more easily resolved.

4. Emotional Intelligence

Daniel Goleman's original concept of Emotional Intelligence has become a valuable tool for explaining the success or failure of relationships.

Communication between the emotional and rational parts of the human brain is the "physical source of emotional intelligence."[3]

However, making good decisions, having a developed *awareness of oneself and others* requires much more. In my opinion, having emotional intelligence means recognizing, accepting and understanding your own—as well as others'—reactions and feelings. This includes being able to monitor and manage your own behavior, make conscious choices and assist others to do the same.

Especially in our primary love relationship, this distinctive aspect of intelligence can help us navigate the inevitable conflicts that every lasting intimate partnership encounters. When issues arise, as they invariably do, a couple's ability to explore realistic solutions, to cooperate, collaborate and reach workable agreements is highly dependent on their emotional intelligence. If at least one of the partners is intelligent emotionally, they are more likely to develop creative "win-win" solutions to their issues.

In certain instances, where a couple has significant conflict and a third-party intervention is required, an emotionally intelligent couple will seek the counsel of an appropriate professional therapist. This can be of great help if and when it's needed. (Part III of this book offers some guidance about choosing a therapist.)

For those of you who are interested in assessing your own emotional intelligence, Travis Bradberry and Jean Greaves in 2004 published *The Emotional Intelligence Quick Book*. Each copy of the book contains a password that enables the reader to go online to take their EQ survey (The Emotional Intelligence Appraisal®).

This can be especially helpful for people who are strongly motivated to increase their sensitivity to others' needs, feelings and perspectives.

5. Repair Statements

In instances where a hurtful argument, external problem or personal upset has caused a rift between partners, there is inevitable pain and disruption. When any relationship has suffered some form of rupture, repair statements are helpful for restoring its emotional health.

Each partner's consciousness and willingness to quickly take responsibility for his/her part in the problem is vital. "Making amends" to repair issues that have created hurt feelings or alienation between you provides fuel for the motor that holds your partnership together.

In fact, making repair statements, apologies and amends

allows both of you to become more vulnerable, more open to intimacy and connection. This builds the potential for a stronger, more secure partnership and deeper levels of trust.

For example, in the case of Devon and Brittany, both needed apologies from the other in order to repair the trust between them following a hateful and vicious argument.

In our therapy session, I was conducting a Sentence Completion exercise, gradually changing the focus to actually making repair statements.

My rigidly structured sentences began with the words, "I feel bad about . . ." Each partner took turns (three or four times) completing this sentence.

Then, as they continued taking turns completing the sentence, I would change the beginning words to:

"I get upset when you . . ."
"I need you to . . ."
"I'm willing to . . ."
"I want us to . . ."
"I'm sorry for saying . . ."
"Please forgive me for . . ."
"I love you because . . ."

As each sentence was completed at least three times by both partners, the spirit between Brittany and Devon began to change.

Brittany quickly became relaxed as the session progressed, while Devon took a bit longer. He needed additional time to learn that Brittany was "not allowed to interrupt" his sentences, the way she "always did." (Likewise, Brittany had to learn to wait her turn and not interrupt him.)

My formal structuring of the sentences created great safety, especially for Devon—male partners often need this more than females.

Trust between them was gradually being rebuilt, as their feelings of love and affection re-emerged.

Susan Campbell and John Grey offer some excellent suggestions for making repair statements in their book, *Five Minute Relationship Repair.* For example, they suggest beginning these statements with phrases like "I reacted because . . ." or "A fear came up in me that . . ." or "A story came up in my mind that triggered . . ." or "What I needed more than anything was to feel . . ." or "If I could do it over I would have . . ."

6. Self-Soothing

Self-soothing is one's own ability to calm down, take a "time out," reflect on upsetting conditions and postpone any reactive behavior.

This type of self-control can greatly lessen the impact of fights or impasses when one or both of you is able to soothe your immediate reactions and potentially overwhelming emotion. As soon as possible it's best to set a time—a "date"—to discuss the issue(s) calmly—preferably within 24 hours.

This postpones the heat of immediate reactivity and allows your rage/disgust to subside until you have time to think about the problem and surrounding circumstances.

Many authors and researchers have noted the value of self-soothing. When this ability becomes a habit, it is a tremendous asset to a relationship. When *both* partners are able to practice self-soothing, the frequency and intensity of conflicts is greatly reduced automatically.

If a couple will agree to a "date" (usually 10 to 15 minutes within the next 24 hours) to revisit an issue, it can usually be dealt with in a calmer and more objective emotional environment.

When this 10-to-15-minute date is insufficient for creating resolution, it's often helpful if the couple can set aside another mutually agreeable time period (such as an hour or two over the weekend) to revisit the problem.

Most of the time our anger, disgust, fear or panic loses its momentum when funneled into an appropriate time and place for expression. This practice of containment, a form of self-soothing, is often an essential ingredient for successful communication.

Strong emotions can evolve into useful and effective aspects of your self, once they are properly contained and expressed.

7. Congruency

Being congruent is essential for honest communication and the building of trust. When you deliver a clear, focused, unambiguous message—one without any double meanings, innuendoes or contradictions—you are being congruent.

But if you're saying one thing and your body language is sending a different message—for example, if you say, "I agree; you're right" while shaking your head "no"—you are being incongruent.

Sometimes being congruent is difficult because we actually have contradictory feelings. When this happens, the most effective (and congruent) approach is to simply stop and attempt to explain your inner conflict.

Incongruent messages resemble a stoplight that turns red and green *at the same time.* If this happened, we'd find it hard to trust the situation and other drivers. It would create a standstill. The same holds true for relationships afflicted with contradictory messages.

8. Compromise

Making compromises, concessions and agreements in a love relationship can sweeten the spirit of the connection and draw a couple closer. However, finding this common ground isn't always easy.

I've often suggested that couples try "chunking" a problem into discrete sections, then dealing with only one "chunk" at a time. There's a well-known martial arts principle called "Yielding to Win." Applying this to the *marital* arts, we see that the more willing and able you are to make concessions, the greater the chances of persuading your partner to adopt your perspective.

Being flexible in your attitude and open to other considerations can be the golden pathway to creating workable compromises.

I'm reminded of a couple in their 50s whom I was seeing for marriage counseling. Their most pressing issue was the direction of their 18-year-old son's career path, and their dilemma seemed unresolvable. The young man wanted to "try out Art School," and he was encouraged in this by his mother.

His dad, however, vehemently objected to financing such a "sissy-ass profession." The father felt his son was "bright enough, strong enough, and accomplished enough academically" to pursue either Law School or Medical School—the only "realistic" choices he could envision for the young man.

Through much "chunking" of the issue into its various parts (e.g., finances; living arrangements; the son's aptitudes and talents, personal motivation, long-term goals and likely consequences) both parents were able to make compromises and concessions that allowed him one full "trial" year at Art School.

He enjoyed the blessing of both parents for that first year and simultaneously gained important insights into his dad's actual motives and concerns for his future.

9. Gratitude

The age-old "attitude of gratitude" is an enormous help in making love thrive. Frequent repetition of such phrases as "Thank you," "I appreciate who you are," and "Thanks for all your help" tend to generate warm feelings, especially in a committed partner.

This feeling of being cherished and acknowledged is essential for the establishment and growth of romantic bonding. It motivates your partner to actually *want* to do the things that please you.

Her/his self-esteem increases, and trust between you deepens.

WHEN IT FAILS

Some love relationships were never meant to last. Perhaps there was only a short-term burst of sexual attraction, or the couple suddenly had to face irreconcilable differences that caught them off guard.

However, when we see deterioration in a relationship that looked promising in the beginning, it's usually because of an accumulation of negative traits. Considerable research is available about the nature of these harmful patterns.

If we were to simply list traits opposite from the nine positive ones discussed in the section above, the new list would spell out a lot of the reasons so many couples fail to create and sustain a loving, functional relationship.

Take a quick look at the following list—this is an overview of "red flags" that often predict the ending of a relationship:

1) The need to be *right* takes over, supported by defensive strategies to control the partner.

2) Certain *"sins of the past"* can never be *forgiven*, forgotten or redefined.

3) There is an *inability* to *discipline and control* one's own actions and reactions (i.e., to play fair, so as not to harm the partner emotionally.)

4) There is a habit of bluntly *interrupting*, speaking out of turn, interrogating, misunderstanding, withdrawing or accusing the partner in the absence of factual evidence.

5) There is a *refusal to take responsibility* for one's own blunders, offenses and transgressions (with no apologies and no effort to repair the damage one has done to the relationship).

6) The *inability to contain one's own emotions* (until an appropriate time and place for their expression) leads to disrupting the partner's equilibrium and sense of and safety.

7) There is a habit of sending *"double messages"* that confuse one's partner about what one is really feeling and thinking.

8) There is an *inability to resolve impasses,* resulting in an insistence that one's own way is the *only* possible option.

9) There is a pattern of *taking the partner for granted,* failing to express appreciation for the partner's contribution to the relationship.

This list represents a condensed version of the most common patterns we see in relationships that are headed for a break-up. Some of these partnerships end quickly; others may continue for years, accumulating pain, insult and resentment along the way.

Thousands of therapists, psychologists, social science researchers, marriage counselors, social workers and others have contributed to the body of knowledge we now have regarding the impediments to lasting romantic relationships.

One I especially respect and admire is John Gottman, one of the most prolific researchers as well as one of the most effective therapists of our time. His many books offer invaluable insights into marriage and relationships. His wide range of subjects includes the factors that predict divorce.

He classifies these destructive relationship factors into four particular categories of negativity that he calls "The Four Horsemen of the Apocalypse":

1) *Criticism*
2) *Contempt*
3) *Defensiveness*
4) *Stonewalling*

These "horsemen" enter the hearts of one or both partners, and if not banished, can bring down the relationship. These four factors cause ever-increasing damage until the undermining culminates in an "apocalypse" that fractures the relationship into divorce.

Let's take a closer look at these four destroyers of love:

1. Criticism

It's important to understand the significant difference between criticism and having a complaint. *Criticism* is global and unspecific. It attacks the partner's personality or character. A *complaint* is not only specific in content and feeling, but also contains a request for what one *does* want. For example:

COMPLAINT: "I'm upset that you didn't stop for groceries. Can you get them later this evening?"

CRITICISM: "You're never responsible! You don't care if we eat or not!"

2. Contempt

Feeling superior to one's partner sets the stage for contempt, which can manifest in sarcasm, expressing disrespect for the partner that poisons the relationship. Gottman contends that "name calling, eye rolling, mockery and hostile humor" all show contempt and/or disgust. Accusations about "moral deficiencies," dressing down the partner and becoming belligerent all play a powerful role in the demise of a romantic relationship.

3. Defensiveness

Blaming one's partner through statements such as "You're the problem, *not me*!" helps goad the other person into escalating the current level of criticism and contempt. Being condescending, making fun of one's partner or putting him/her down in a subtle way are also forms of defensiveness. The implied message here is: "I'm agitated and frustrated because of *you*. So don't blame *me*!"

4. Stonewalling

When criticism, contempt and defensiveness build up to an unbearable level, one of the partners shuts down, refusing to engage on any level, i.e., stonewalling. He/she is opting out of painful feelings, fights, and ultimately the relationship with the mate.

Both Gottman and fellow-researcher Simon Baron-Cohen see stonewalling as more common among men, who are more easily "flooded" with overwhelming emotion than women are. Females have a tendency to become hyper-verbal and hysterical in a conflict; this pushes males into the fight-or-flight response of stonewalling, in which they take "flight" from the woman's barrage of verbal assault. If she persists in piling on the verbiage, he may flip over into the "fight" reaction, which is likely to be far more destructive.

While in a "flight" reaction (i.e., stonewalling) men feel safer. They usually refuse eye contact and offer no form of physical or verbal acknowledgment, acting as if they don't care. They cannot relax enough to talk until they feel safe in the environment.

Gottman has observed that when these four patterns or some combination of them become predictable and consistent within a relationship or marriage, the union is almost bound to fail (especially in the absence of skillful therapeutic intervention).

I have personally worked with hundreds of couples in whose relationship some combination of these "horsemen" is present. I've also found that—when an empathic understanding of the partner evolves, it can pave the way for effective and loving communication to emerge. This is the goal of successful therapy. But of course it cannot always be the outcome.

In a minority of cases, couples decide that "therapy" is not worth the effort—the time, money and painful unraveling of underlying issues.

In most cases where we do achieve success, both partners feel the work was worth the struggle. In order to excavate the deeper wounds of childhood, certain skills need to be developed during therapy, including active listening; self-disclosure; building trust and a sense of safety; and making connections that had not been previously recognized.

Sometimes the damage caused by parents, caregivers or society itself cut so deeply into the fabric of personality and character that even the most insightful and heroic efforts of therapists fail. Also, in a minority of cases, the once deeply felt romantic love between partners may have simply died along the way.

In most cases, however, such huge therapeutic effort pays off. The once-felt passion and attraction, fragile though it may have seemed, often springs to life again.

LEVEL OF WOUNDEDNESS

As any experienced therapist can tell you, one of the most accurate predictors of relationship failure is the degree of psychological damage created in childhood.

The concept of the "Imago" as developed by Harville Hendrix in *Getting the Love You Want* helps explain such damage to the psyche.

Our image (i.e., the Imago) of our "right mate" becomes our quest. This imagined partner, through becoming our mate, will—we assume—help us fill in our "disowned" self—the missing parts that have caused us to feel empty or incomplete.

We all yearn for the wholeness, safety and joy that we felt as young children. Finding our "perfect soul mate" (the lover who will heal our wounds, fill in our lost parts) will allow us, we believe, to complete our self and so become whole again.

Hendrix explains that the Imago, our image of our right mate, is unconsciously formed as a composite of the traits—both *positive* and *negative*—of our immediate caretakers (usually our parents). Although these people are most often the mother and father, in some cases they could be siblings, grandparents, close relatives, nannies, etc.

Hendrix observes that the **negative** traits are the most influential, the most remembered, and the **deepest wounds**. We naturally seek to heal these wounds, to feel whole and safe. It is in the crucible of love relationships that this healing might take place. And so we develop the composite ideal for our perfect soul mate— the one whose love can heal our wounds and bring closure and relief to our hearts.

The childhood experiences that threatened our existence, the ones most deeply recorded, were the ones that wounded us most. Much of the time we are painfully—and dangerously—unaware of how these *negative* traits operate in our psyche and determine our attraction patterns.

FINDING THE PERFECT SOULMATE

In my own clinical practice, a common scenario that demonstrates this is the profile of a capable young woman whom I'll call Cindy. Raised by an abusive alcoholic father, Cindy desperately wanted her "ideal mate" to achieve sobriety, become sensitive and loving, and regard her feelings and needs as real. This is her Imago, her composite picture of the people who impacted her most in early childhood and who now comprise her ideal mate.

By the time Cindy came to me for therapy, she was devastated that her last three relationships had "all ended in some form of abuse while the guy was drunk." It took a while for her to see that her deepest need was to get the abusive alcoholic to **become sober** and **learn how to love her.** She was naturally attracted to the situation through which this could happen (the drunken boyfriend who needed rescuing and sobriety).

Unfortunately, none of the men Cindy felt "chemistry" for was remotely interested in *sobriety.* She slowly came to realize that a healthy mate for her would be a man who had *already* become sober, on his own, and was interested in loving her (without the help of any mind-altering substances).

The process of excavating Cindy's Imago and her lovemap (the combination of qualities she needed in a romantic partner) was immensely painful. But her breakthrough into the freedom to seek out a *sober mate* was worth the struggle. She slowly moved away from her original (unconsciously based) image of the "perfect soul mate" as an alcoholic who would love her more than he loved his addiction. Her revised image (now fully conscious) was of an attraction to sober men, who were capable of loving her with no baggage of addiction to impede their whole-heartedness.

The grueling process of changing Cindy's "ideal mate" image from an unhealthy version to a healthy one was the goal of therapy; actual changes in a person's lovemap are extremely difficult to make.

In most relationships, there are understandable feelings of hopelessness and misery when our partner fails to help us heal our deepest wounds and recover the true self we had to "disown" in childhood in order to survive.

GOOD MATCHES

When our mate is a *"good match,"* the stage is set for us to heal some of our most grievous wounds. Even for individuals like Cindy, saddled with self-defeating images of their "ideal mate," solutions can appear, either through intensive therapy or, occasionally, through extremely good luck in finding a psychologically healthy mate with whom love can deepen on its own.

In many cases, couples are actually *"weak matches"* for each other's idealized images of the perfect mate. Sometimes they foster illusions about their partner until there is such dissatisfaction and disappointment that the relationship falls apart. They break up or get divorced because they've run out of interest and energy to make it work. "Weak matches" often result in people saying, "We grew apart; I knew there was someone better for me." or "There's just no chemistry."

WEAK MATCHES

Many "weakly matched" couples somehow create conditions that make genuine intimacy impossible. Hendrix lists all kinds of avoidance tactics, ranging from "disappearing into the garage" to having affairs and refusing to make love.

When romantic love transforms into everyday reality, many people feel disappointed and angry. So they turn elsewhere—to hobbies, to cuddly pets, to affairs, to obsessions over their children—anything to avoid facing the fact that they are *not* taking pleasure in one another. The fear arises that their deepest needs will never be met and that, therefore, their deepest wounds (usually unconscious) will never be healed. Each partner, separately and silently, harbors her/his own despair over this realization.

Unfortunately, many couples never get the therapeutic help they need—which may range anywhere from formal marriage counseling to the use of some or all of the *Tools* in this book. Many painful and dysfunctional relationships could not only be saved but could become genuinely happy if the couple were open to the help that is readily available.

• Betrayal •

In their book, *What Makes Love Last*, Gottman and Silver take on the task of defining various forms of betrayal that constitute a clear move toward the demise of any love relationship. These include:

1) Compulsive use of pornography (not shared with the partner).

2) Sexual and non-sexual affairs (where honest commitment to the partner is sacrificed).

3) Lying: deceit for any reason.

4) Forming coalitions with others to "gang up" on the partner.

5) Absenteeism: not being "present"—physically, emotionally or both.

6) Withdrawal of personal and/or sexual interest.

7) Disrespect or implication that the partner is inferior to oneself.

8) Taking advantage of the partner—being unfair.

9) Self-centeredness, selfishness: the inability to set aside one's own needs for the "common good" of the relationship.

10) Breaking promises or agreements.

There are many additional forms of betrayal, all of which are relationship-killers. The point is to bring these patterns to *conscious awareness* so as to deal with them openly and honestly —whether alone or in private counseling sessions. Betrayal invariably paves the way for dissolving a relationship if solid trust is not rebuilt.

• Detachment and Denial •

In *The Relationship Cure*, an earlier book co-authored with Joan De Claire, Gottman also does an excellent job of explaining how detachment and denial become destroyers of committed relationships. Unfortunately, our American culture offers many self-help books, TV shows and role models that actually encourage detachment.

Our media, pop culture and advertising reflect little awareness of the despair, pain and remorse that many individuals suffer over their relationships.

Yet the most satisfying and fulfilling relationships are those that encompass a full range of emotions, including the negative ones. Gottman, like me, believes the capacity for this kind of *vulnerability* is part of being fully human, since it allows us to bond more deeply with a partner or spouse—or even a close friend.

Sharing our anger/betrayal/terror/disgust/fear/shock/shame/sorrow might feel risky in the moment; yet it is the process of *sharing these extreme feelings* that brings us closer in our emotional bonding with others.

Whatever psychological pain and trauma each of us has endured—especially in our deepest wounds from childhood—it is our personal *responsibility* to understand how these negative events created our "hot buttons," fears and long-term vulnerabilities. By denying or detaching from these wounds, we inevitably set the stage for assuming our relationship problems will be impossible to resolve. Only by taking the risks involved in being fully present, vulnerable and self-disclosing can we pave the way for healthy intimacy.

MALE AND FEMALE BRAINS

In any in-depth study of love relationships, it's helpful to consider the biology, the DNA structure of the differences between men and women. This knowledge alone can explain many of our heartaches, miscommunications and baffling frustrations with the "opposite" sex.

The groundbreaking contribution of Simon Baron-Cohen

in *The Essential Difference* established a new awareness among psychologists that the basic differences between the sexes account for far more of our misunderstandings and conflicts than we previously believed.

His brilliant research makes clear how the *"female brain"* is configured to access great empathy, verbal skills, an ability to read body language and a gift for building emotional relationships. The *"male brain,"* in contrast, is configured to speak plainly—using as few words as possible—and to build systems. (Think engineers, surgeons, draftsmen, architects, computer experts, mechanics, composers, and musicians.)

Of course we all know the exceptions—men whose gift for empathy and other "female" specialties makes them superb caregivers, counselors, nurses and child-care experts. We also know women who have had impressive careers in male-dominated professions.

It's also true, however, that many men are puzzled that their female partners seem happy sitting for hours with other women, talking about feelings and relationships or "just gossiping." And quite a few women are perplexed to see their male partners spending hours puttering alone in the garage building a shelf or repairing a bicycle.

As a child, I often wondered how Dad knew how everything worked and could fix anything that got broken. Mom, also true to her gender, did most of the talking—with girlfriends, neighbors and relatives. She was the one everyone went to for help when their feelings got hurt or when they had a fight with someone. It was an effective division of labor: Dad fixed all the mechanical things, while Mom fixed all the emotional upsets.

Of course Baron-Cohen recognizes that many people's biological gender is at odds with the statistical averages of things most individuals of their gender like to do and can do well. But in families like mine the brains of Mom and Dad were pretty close to the norms Baron-Cohen observed in our society.

It seems there's no way to avoid recognizing that these general differences between women and men account for many of the relationship crises, breakdowns and communication lapses that I've seen so often professionally in my couples' therapy sessions.

Naïve couples who fall in love sometimes assume that their mate will be similar to them, see things their way and share their intense interests. Given what we now know about the different dynamics of male and female brains, it's understandable that some of these couples are in for serious disappointment.

Many of the marriage counseling sessions in my private practice have been devoted mainly to educating couples on the differences between male and female brains that I've summarized above. These couples are now able to avoid fighting over these issues, thanks to the new insights gained through their therapy sessions. Suddenly, they see why so many self-help books have been written to assist couples overwhelmed by the reality of these differences (John Grey's popular *Men Are from Mars, Women Are from Venus*, is an excellent example).

• About Women •

Many love relationships are radically improved when the female partner comes to realize that her talent for empathy, her comfort with intense emotions and her gift for conversation may never be matched by her male partner.

Biology has dealt us women a tricky (and sometimes disappointing) hand. Men, as a rule, simply don't have the empathy skills necessary to engage in the kind of conversation that we frequently enjoy with girlfriends. After some of my long, satisfying talks with a woman friend, my husband, Eddie, would often ask me, "What did you guys do?" My response was usually, "We just talked—had a fabulous time." His incredulous face expressed his inability to imagine *anyone* spending over three hours "just talking."

For most women—and a few unusual men—the process of sharing feelings, talking about emotions and relationships is *an end in itself.* It has inherent value and offers great satisfaction to people who have a predominantly "female" brain.

Baron-Cohen reports that, by the age of six, 99 percent of girls—compared with only 17 percent of boys—play with dolls. Playing with dolls requires a high level of imagining what Mommy and the doll are feeling and needing—all building toward intensifying caring, deepening emotional ties with others and developing a high level of empathy.

When a young woman falls in love with a potential mate, her heart yearns for *reciprocity,* and she focuses on mutual emotions. In many instances, her heart is broken when the typical male's preoccupation with showing his physical strength, prowess and dominance prevail. He often assumes that she will value his accomplishments and superior strength in the same way he does. In reality, she is often deeply hurt that he isn't as interested as she is in developing the close, caring ties she has spent her whole life preparing to savor. It becomes clear that he *isn't as sensitive to others' feelings as she is.*

This chasm in the biological differences between the sexes and their resulting predispositions often produces breakdowns in communication, wrenching misunderstandings, and a profound sense of alienation for both partners. A typical outcome: "We're breaking up, because (he/she) just doesn't care about *me.*"

Along with the female brain's general superiority at empathizing, it also has greater language skills and capacity for verbal memory. This blockbuster combination intimidates many men, who tend to respond: "I refuse to argue with her! I just can't win."

Thus, in response to increasing verbal demands from his female partner that he is unable either to cope with or to match, he simply "stonewalls."

Most of the time, women are able to **out-argue** their male partners and overwhelm them with verbal opinions and explanations. This often pushes the male into **complete shutdown** and disconnection—discussed earlier in relation to the "stonewalling" that is the last of Gottman's "Four Horsemen of the Apocalypse"—and a predictor of divorce.

• About Men •

Just as most women are better at empathizing and verbalizing, men are usually superior at what Baron-Cohen calls *"systemizing"* (i.e., an affinity for systems and how they work, combined with a gift for building them). We see practical applications of this talent in the work of chemists, mechanical engineers, surgeons, astronomers, architects, and many others.

This special gift of the *"male brain"* also manifests itself in such fields as coaching sports teams, military strategy, logic, music theory, physics, computer programming and rocket design.

The male brain's natural focus on such pursuits distracts him from "relationship maintenance"—the empathy and emotional sensitivity so vital to his female mate.

This is one of the reasons most women turn to girlfriends for deep and meaningful "talks." Even when the subject of these conversations is not particularly "meaningful," the very process of verbal exchange creates in the participants a sense of warmth and caring.

Many researchers and social scientists have observed that infant boys pick cars, trucks, and building blocks to play with—showing no interest in available dolls.

On the whole, even cross-culturally, we observe one- day-old boys staring longer at mechanical objects than at human faces. You should have no difficulty in guessing what one-day-old girls focus on. Yes, human faces—even including silent "talking heads" on a television screen.

As adults, women are better prepared to state their hurts and grievances, while men are often unsure of exactly *what* they feel. Even when men do become aware of their own negative feelings, they often erupt in anger or simply state the problem and withdraw contact—rather than trying to "fix" the relationship with further "talking" (which they often feel *caused* the problem, to begin with).

Men are generally prone to speak in **direct commands**—a shortcut for getting the job done. Many researchers—including John Grey, Harville Hendrix, John Gottman and Simon Baron-Cohen—have confirmed this pattern. Such commands (e.g., "Don't do that" or "Give that to me" or "Silence, please") can sound domineering and frequently cause the female partner to feel disrespected or uncared for. Here is one juncture where conflict can easily erupt—and often does.

Women—even very young girls—generally use "socially en-abling" language that is inclusive. They encourage the expression of different perspectives, pause to give others an opportunity to speak, and take turns speaking, etc.

All these techniques use intimacy and empathy to encourage the formation of a bonding experience.

Men, on the other hand, tend to use language to display their knowledge, skill, dominance and/or superior status. Their gestures are clearly not intended to promote the intimacy and/or bonding that the "female brain" prefers.

RELATIONSHIP SURVIVAL

What a satisfying experience it is to see a couple study these differences, gain meaningful empathy with each other and open the way for a deeper romantic love to thrive.

However, this takes not only *commitment* to the relationship but also some *time* scheduled into a couple's busy lives. Contemporary culture offers us many diversions and opportunities to avoid this kind of relationship enrichment. Thus, taking the 15 or 20 minutes (in some cases longer) to complete one of the exercises in Part II of this book can feel like too much effort, especially if one feels uncertain about the outcome.

As we've seen, understanding the two "different brains" can account for much of our distress with the "opposite" sex. Typically, a man feels pushed emotionally to "talk"—a battle he expects to lose. A woman is more likely to feel discounted and neglected when her male partner refuses to deal with her emotions. This is a moment when a fight or serious argument is likely to ensue—threatening to further undermine their "love" relationship.

The 10 *Tools* offered in the next section of this book provide the structure and pathway for couples to embark on a journey of relationship enrichment and healing.

It's with this in mind that I've decided to share these precisely chosen *Tools* to facilitate the process. In some instances, where professional help (therapy, marriage counseling) is needed, Part III deals with some criteria you and your partner may want to consider.

• Who Can Benefit from Part II — The Tools •

The heart of this book, Part II, is a selection of *10 Tools* designed to assist any couple that is committed to making their love grow and mature.

As with most patterns in our lives, the reported happiness of romantic partners can be displayed on a "bell curve" graph that shows the happiest 15 percent on one end and the unhappiest 15 percent at the other. The remaining 70 percent of couples form the bell-shaped "hump" at the center of the graph.

It is primarily for this 70 percent that I offer the *10 Tools*; this group is the most likely to find these exercises of particular value to help deepen their already workable relationship.

Take, for example, Kate and Jim. Married for six years, basically happy together, they are in their early 30s and have two sons, ages 2 and 4. Both partners were feeling stressed by the daily demands of parenthood and a dual-career lifestyle.

Tensions consistently mounted on most evenings after dinner. The boys needed their final playtime, and after that needed to be bathed. Dirty dishes had piled up, bills needed paying and laundry needed to be done.

One evening Kate burst into tears and said, "I just can't do it all!"

Jim was caught off-guard by her complaint, since he saw himself as a devoted, "hands-on" dad. He played games and wrestled with the boys for hours, but assumed that Kate would prefer to bathe them, as she'd done since they were infants. Jim routinely got the house "picked up" so that he and Kate could have some romantic time together after the boys were asleep.

With the use of only *one* of the *Tools* (*#3*: "Love Styles"), Kate and Jim were able to reduce much of their cumulative stress.

Jim was surprised that Kate rated *"Acts of Service"* as her number one priority (while he rated *"Quality Time"* as his).

Offering many examples, Kate explained to Jim that, while she appreciated his playing with the boys, she needed him to "cut it short" so *he* could bathe the boys and get them into bed. She told him she didn't mind doing the dishes alone, then paying whatever bills were due and taking care of the laundry.

As they discussed their needs further and put their new "evening program" in place, their tensions seemed to dissolve. Both reported feeling deeply happy as they read the boys stories together and turned off the lights.

There is nothing inherently magical about *Tool #3*. It was Jim who suggested they try this exercise that friends had sent to them. What made the difference for this couple was the respectful and supportive attitudes both brought to the task of easing their "cumulative tension."

Even with all the pressures Kate and Jim were experiencing, they were clearly in the 15 percent of the "happiest couples." They enjoyed a mutual sense of trust and safety, and they felt no need to defend their own preferences or criticize each other. Their ability to nurture one another and pursue mutual goals was exceptional.

This couple offers an example of how the *Tools* can be of significant help. Kate and Jim had no need for professional intervention because their relationship already had a strong foundation.

• When the Road Is Really Rough •

In contrast, consider the case of Will and Cassidy. Married for five years, both 33, they had no children together (although Will had fathered a child with a previous girlfriend). Trust between these two was almost nonexistent, and their communication was filled with blaming, shaming and stonewalling. Cassidy was chronically frustrated with Will's pattern of *abusing her verbally,* then lapsing into *stony silence* and refusing to acknowledge her existence. She reacted to his behavior with intense feelings of *alienation, hopelessness* and *contempt,* which she expressed through frequent screaming, crying and name-calling. In the face of this, Will felt justified in leaving their home and re-involving himself in a torrid sexual affair that he had been indulging in for the past three years.

By the time they sought counseling from me, lying and infidelity had become standard procedure for Will, while *hysteria, low self-esteem* and *depression* had become Cassidy's daily emotional state. There was a striking absence of warmth, caring and support between them.

As I interviewed each of them separately, it became clear that Will had no respect for Cassidy and was using her outbursts and name-calling to justify his ongoing affair. Her levels of contempt and defensiveness were rapidly growing. All romantic feelings between them had been extinguished.

Although Cassidy had no conscious knowledge of Will's long-term affair, she summed up their relationship, saying, "He's not the man I thought I'd married."

It was clear to me that this marriage was over—or at least might soon be. Although each of them derived some sadistic pleasure from blaming and shaming the other, it was time to call a halt to their accusations and insults and move on to "damage control."

I explained how serious psychological injury can be inflicted on a partner when there is such a stark absence of trust, good will, safety, caring and civil communication between them. It was time, I said, for both of them to "call it quits"—back off and get some relief. Any further counseling sessions, I suggested, should be focused on getting a "successful divorce"— i.e., one that involved a minimum of damage to both partners.

Will and Cassidy were in the 15 percent of "unhappiest" couples, and any attempt to help them use the *Tools* would have been a waste of time. Their relationship was what we sometimes call D.O.A. (Dead-on-Arrival in therapy).

This "unhappiest" 15 percent of couples are the least likely to be helped by the *Tools,* and the reason is obvious. The *Tools* themselves are based on the assumption that, regardless of the problems a couple may have, the underlying relationship is *fundamentally strong.* Their issues with lack of empathy, knowledge and insight; value conflicts; stress; control issues and/or defense mechanisms can be overcome—if love and commitment are still part of the foundation of their partnership.

This criterion for probable effectiveness of the *Tools* applies also to the 85 percent of couples who make up the "middle" and "happiest" portions of the relationship bell curve. Even partners in the "happiest 15 percent" can benefit from these *Tools*, as we saw with Kate and Jim, since stress and failures of communication sometimes afflict us all—not just young couples struggling to cope with the demands of two careers and young children.

However, the most dramatic gains from the *Tools* have been reported by the 70 percent of couples in the central "hump" of the bell curve. For this group the new insights and information available through the *Tools* can greatly improve the quality of a marriage or committed partnership—especially when issues related to crucial decisions—religious practices, career choices, relations with in-laws, finances and health decisions are involved.

As a result of doing even one or two of the exercises in Part II, many couples have reported significant insights, greater empathy and deeper intimacy with their partners. Your love relationship is probably the most important one of your adult life, and anything you can do to enhance it is well worth your time and energy.

I hope you and your partner benefit greatly from using the *10 Tools,* and that they help the love you already have to grow and thrive.

— PART II —

THE TEN TOOLS

1   **UNDERPINNINGS:**
Six Qualities to Help Love Thrive

2   **LOVE, LIKING AND LUST:**
What Shape Is Your Triangle?

3   **LOVE STYLES:**
Different Ways of Giving Love

4   **INTIMACY RATING:**
How Do You Score?

5   **BATTLE BETWEEN THE SEXES:**
Guidelines for Getting It

6   **GETTING TO KNOW YOU:**
Sentence Completion

7   **SUBTYPES:**
The Hidden Level of Personality

8   **COMPATIBILITY RATING:**
How Compatible Are You?

9   **RESOLVING CONFLICT:**
Turning Right

10   **ATTITUDE AND MINDSET:**
Finding a Different Street

1

UNDERPINNINGS:
Six Qualities to Help Love Thrive

Over my many years of counseling couples, one central question has consistently emerged. Ultimately, one way or another, clients would ask, "If we sincerely want to create a happy, successful marriage [or, in many cases, "a deep intimate relationship"], what do we need to do?" "What does it take?"

This is a complex question. It's especially difficult to answer, realizing how distinctive each couple is. Each has different circumstances, personal problems, various combinations of personality types and divergent backgrounds and cultures—to list only a few of the significant factors they may face.

In pursuit of a helpful response, I studied the relationships of highly successful, happy, stable couples—and tried to put together a list of the essential elements that produced these exceptionally satisfying relationships.

My efforts resulted in a list of six qualities that appear to underlie the habits and attitudes of these special couples:

1) Commitment
2) Safety
3) Trust

4) Open communication

5) Empathy/Knowledge

6) Nurturing

For each quality, I'll discuss some exceptions, where professional therapy was required. In these cases, the *Tools*, when used alone, were *insufficient* to help the couple resolve their dilemmas. Please remember, these actual clinical cases were truly the *exceptions,* not the general rule, since many other couples were able to use the *Tools* effectively, unaided. (Although every case developed exactly as I present it here, all *names* have been changed to insure anonymity.)

These are examples of how clients actually used *Tool #1* in therapy, demonstrating how one or more of the *Six Qualities* was either weak or missing.

(At the same time many couples used this *Tool* effectively on their own outside of formal therapy.)

1. Commitment— "No Exit" Decision

A young woman I'll call Gloria (age 28, married for two years) was continually threatening her husband, Lester, with "divorce" or "separation" because he wasn't quite ready to have their first child. Gloria had been coached by her mother to "Keep him on his toes—always afraid you might leave him."

Gloria actually felt no desire for any kind of separation. Her mother's bad advice served only to make Lester feel Gloria wasn't committed to him or their marriage. It was time for Gloria to put her mother's "advice" on the "back burner" and assure Lester of her love and commitment.

Another example: Merrilee and Alex, a charming, highly compatible couple in their early 40s, both working as artists, had lived together for almost 20 years without giving in to social pressure to marry. They had expressed pride about not needing any "legal papers" to make their relationship work.

But for the last year Merrilee had begun to worry about health insurance, inheritance rights, powers-of-attorney, the necessity to make wills and perhaps create a Living Trust. Every time she tried to approach Alex about these concerns, he would get "stoned" on marijuana. He passively refused to be "present" (sober) to discuss these issues with her directly. Although she had no desire for "legal marriage," she was painfully aware of the many potential legal problems that could arise. She simply wanted to take the appropriate steps. Alex's inability to remain sober even for a conversation with her about this issue clearly demonstrated his lack of *commitment* to fortify the permanence of their relationship.

2. Safety

I believe that almost everyone wants to feel both physically and emotionally safe with his/her partner. But in some cases this can seem impossible, and the situation needs resolution.

In one case, I vividly recall Mason, the husband, saying he "never felt safe during sex," which seemed odd given the petite stature of his wife, Ellen. I learned that she had been forcibly date-raped in college, with the perpetrator trying to silence her by holding a hand over her mouth. Once, while they were making love, Mason tried to hush her verbally, concerned about waking their two young children in the adjoining room. She suffered a sudden flashback to the rape and was so violently triggered that she began beating her husband with her fists.

Shocked by her fierceness, Mason ran into the bathroom, fearful of responding in kind and possibly hurting her. His feeling of being physically unsafe with her led him to seek my help for counseling.

Ellen was able to do some short-term individual therapy and resolve her repressed rage. Mason was greatly relieved that her flashbacks could actually be resolved; he felt safe once again.

In another, less dramatic case, an older couple in their mid-60s with grown children came to see me because Margaret had been complaining for years that she "didn't matter" to her husband, Lenny, and that she was "always invisible" to him. He protested that this was not true.

As I explored their backgrounds, it became clear that cultural differences played a major part in their apparent impasse. Lenny's Japanese mother had raised him with strict rules about "manners." In the Japanese culture it is considered rude and intrusive to look another person directly in the eye. Lenny's lifelong attempt to honor this rule had contributed to his introverted personality and made him appear aloof to many people.

Margaret, raised in a typical American household, understood Lenny's reticence and loved him for the kind and loyal husband he had been all these years. Yet she could no longer tolerate the complete lack of eye contact between them, which made her feel "shut out."

As the three of us explored this situation, Lenny came to realize that what he thought of as "non-invasive" behavior had made his beloved wife feel "invisible." It was clear that he loved her dearly and was devastated at having caused her emotional pain. He willingly worked out a plan to change his habits.

3. Trust

This is a central issue for healthy relationships. It is essential that each partner believe the other will follow through on agreements and promises. We all need to feel confident that our partner has been completely honest and straightforward with us, even—maybe especially—when we wish things could be different.

Most couples say they would rather work with the "whole truth" than with half-truths or deceptions. Most people have experienced giving or receiving "white lies" to "spare the feelings" of their spouses or partners. Sometimes these don't seem to matter much; at other times they can break the heart and betray the trust of the loved one.

Truth can be an awkward and, at times, painful reality. Each person needs to consider the consequences of sharing or not sharing certain information with the partner. In some cases, it can be so destructive and unnerving to the partner that it may be better left unsaid (providing it is *not* essential to the welfare or the future of the partner).

I'm reminded of a few examples of couples' dilemmas where a certain revelation was either unnecessary or irrelevant.

In one excruciating situation, a young wife named Deborah (age 25, married almost one year) was a devout Catholic. Her beloved and loyal husband, Martin, was also devoted to their shared faith and deeply involved in the "Right to Life" anti-abortion movement. His stance was that "No woman should ever consider abortion, regardless of the circumstances," and Deborah basically agreed with him.

However, she was concealing a deep secret, something she had never told anyone but her own mother. At age 16 she had been seduced by an aggressive 21-year-old guy—her first and only sexual experience before her marriage to Martin. She became pregnant from this encounter, never saw her seducer again, and told only her mother (also a devout Catholic) about her predicament. Together, she and her mother decided, after considerable research, that she would go out of state, use a fictitious name and get a safe, therapeutic abortion. They agreed that going through with childbirth would ruin Deborah's future, since there was no way she could raise a child at age 16.

She and her mom decided together that they would keep this secret for life. They chose not to tell Deborah's dad, since he was radically anti-abortion and she was terrified of his potential reaction.

After she and her mother had kept this secret for over nine years, Deborah came to see me, distressed about not wanting her marriage to be "based on a lie" but fearful of destroying the marriage if she told her husband the truth.

Such dilemmas need to be resolved, keeping in mind the highest good for all concerned. This is the kind of situation in which professional counseling can assist a person (or couple) to clarify her/his options and potential consequences. (Under no circumstances should the therapist project her/his personal opinions or values onto such situations.)

Most situations involving trust are not as complicated as Deborah's and can be resolved by the couple themselves through *open communication.* In this case, after extensive discussion with her mother and me, Deborah decided to continue keeping this particular lifelong secret between herself and her mother.

Another case involved an adventurous young married couple, Tina and Hal, who were presented with an opportunity to explore "swinging" (or wife-swapping). A friend of Hal's told him about a club he and his wife belonged to, where members were invited to parties at which opportunities for sex with other members' spouses were available (all with polite permission, of course).

Hal told Tina about this "club," and they discussed whether this was something they would want to explore. They decided together that breaking their vow of monogamy might be so traumatic that it wasn't worth the risk. They felt that if ever their vow of strict monogamy were compromised (even by mutual consent), the solid trust they had established with each other might be damaged. They agreed that no amount of sexual adventure could be worth that potential loss, and they decided to decline Hal's friend's invitation.

4. Open Communication

Given all of our cultural rules about good manners and propriety, plus the common fear of rejection, it's a wonder that any couple actually communicates openly with both 1) *self-disclosure* and 2) *active listening.*

It's helpful for most people to examine in depth these two aspects. First, it's imperative that the "sender" present clear and honest messages, avoiding those that manipulate answers by their very nature. Certain questions, for example, contain built-in accusations: "When did you learn about your abuse?" "How many times have you lied about this?" These manipulative quasi-inquiries are simply variations on the classic "When did you stop beating your wife?"

Genuine *self-disclosure* usually involves self-revealing and honest statements. The information is clear, concise and not designed to produce some desired outcome from the partner.

The other side of Open Communication is *active listening* on the part of each partner. This involves summarizing what your partner has said, with clarity about his/her intended meaning and attitude. This "mirroring" (i.e., accurate reflection) of your partner's message is free of any of your personal opinions, value judgments or defenses.

For example, if your partner discloses that she/he is upset with you, it's important to mirror back accurately, beginning with the four words "I heard you say. . . . For example, "I heard you say you're upset with me because . . . (you summarize their reason(s); here you are incorporating your partner's real feelings, attitude and meaning).

If the speaker is not satisfied that you heard his/her meaning correctly, the process is *repeated* until the listener "gets it right." Then the two of you *take turns* being 1) the sender/self-discloser and 2) the receiver/ active listener. The process of formal listening is highly structured and is designed both to insure accuracy in the receiver "getting the message" and to provide assurance to the sender that the message was received correctly.

This method of Open Communication is ***not about agreement, debate or validity.*** The process of "active listening" is only about being present so that the listener can feed back what was said with *100-percent accuracy.* "Taking turns," once the sender of the message indicates, "That's right," insures that both parties have an equal chance to clearly send their message, and the *listener* has a calm, unbiased arena in which he/she can listen effectively.

5. Empathy/Knowledge
This involves taking the time and making the effort to acquire a deep understanding of your mate. This requires you to acquire some significant knowledge about your partner's fears, desires, goals, motivations, frustrations and past traumas. No wonder a long period of "engagement" is often recommended for couples.

Acquiring knowledge-in-depth about your partner requires experiencing together the daily "bumps" of trauma, disappointment, holidays, in-laws, money issues—and perhaps an illness or accident that truly tests the responses and resiliency of you both—not only as individuals but also as a couple functioning as a team.

I'm reminded of a couple in their late 40s (basically happy, with two kids in college) who came to see me with a "sudden crisis." Jennifer was so upset with her husband, Clyde, she couldn't sustain any eye contact with him. He was aghast at her extreme lack of empathy and kindness toward him; she had never behaved like this before.

She had planned a 5-day "surprise" trip to Hawaii with their best friends (two couples they had enjoyed traveling with before). The six of them were to stay together on a large houseboat that the wives had rented at an amazingly reasonable price. What was there not to like about this? All the arrangements and tickets had been taken care of (routine tasks that Clyde disliked, anyhow).

But he kept "digging in his heels" making excuses about why he couldn't go, and finally—in an irrational "fit"—proclaimed, "I won't go. Period!"

Jennifer was at her wits' end; never, in their "22 years of a good marriage" had anything like this ever happened. Her despair was evident, and so was his.

As I dug deeply into Clyde's motives, questioning almost everything, he suddenly burst out with uncontrollable sobbing. We eventually discovered that at the age of 4, when spending a week on a houseboat with his mother and new stepfather, he came very close to drowning. His falling overboard—and feeling totally helpless and abandoned by both adults— became a totally *repressed trauma* in his subconscious. He would have drowned, if not for a rescue by houseboat neighbors who happened to be trained paramedics on vacation themselves. Obviously, Clyde survived, but told himself he would *never* do this again, or even think about it, *ever.*

He managed to so totally repress his feelings and fears that he was successful in achieving complete denial about the incident. In the couple's busy 22 years of marriage, raising their children and putting them through college, there had never been an opportunity for a "houseboat vacation" until right now.

It *wasn't* that he was hiding this trauma from Jennifer; he "actually hadn't thought about it since around age 10." Now he was petrified.

With this new knowledge, Jennifer quickly called a meeting with the other two couples, explained the situation, and asked if they would agree to exchange the houseboat for a beach cottage.

One of the other wives had also expressed apprehension about "the boat." Everyone strongly supported their request, displaying a deep degree of empathy. Jennifer met with the travel agent, and plans were quickly changed to a lovely four-bed-room beach cottage (at a slightly lower price). Everyone was happy.

This is a clear example of how *empathy* and *knowledge* can clear the way for a love relationship to flourish. Both of the other couples, as well as Clyde's wife, were completely willing to honor his request and, in fact, enjoyed the change. Everyone displayed deep empathy.

Taking the time to really *know your partner* is essential; putting yourself in his/her shoes is far more demanding. Empathy is extremely difficult—often impossible—to teach. Unlike the couples in this example, some people simply lack the ability to empathize with others. This disability can be extremely dangerous in a love relationship.

In another case, Marilyn, the wife of a prominent doctor came to me in desperation because her husband "just refused" to see her point of view on "almost everything." George was a highly intelligent and honest man who was rigid and dogmatic in his opinions. For example, he was insisting that their college-age daughter "go into the sciences," and refused to discuss her burning desire to attend art school. Similarly, he could not understand his wife's devotion to her "silly card club" and her "unnecessary shopping dates" with close girlfriends.

The marriage ended—peacefully, in divorce, but with a total lack of empathy on George's part (perhaps a case of Asperger's Syndrome). He had no desire to change.

6. Nurturing

This is the ability to assist one's partner to achieve what *she/he* wants and to ultimately become more fully who she/he really is— to *self-actualize*.

Like empathy, real nurturing involves **getting your own ego out of the way** (i.e., what you want, what you feel, what you believe) so that you can facilitate the growth and well-being of your partner. This can be extremely difficult—and completely impossible if you are feeling threatened or envious at the time. Insecurity may not only block any form of empathy but can also paralyze your ability to actually nurture your partner.

One case that demonstrates this inability to nurture the partner is that of Dave and Connie—married 29 years, with twin boys who had recently graduated with master's degrees in Engineering and secured promising career positions.

Dave and Connie had worked hard all their lives, and both had only high school educations. Dave was a successful electrician, and Connie a top-notch legal secretary.

Now, at age 53, Connie decided that she really wanted to go to college. Her desire was to become a Social Worker specializing in adoptions, or perhaps work for a non-profit Foundation. She craved the challenge and potential satisfaction of a career she had chosen for herself.

Dave was angry; he was extremely upset that Connie would "even think about going to college at age 53." He felt she was "crazy to sacrifice her high salary as a legal secretary." He also felt extremely threatened: What would she do next? Who would she meet at college? What then?

He ended up forbidding Connie to quit her job. In one of our counseling sessions he refused to support her through college. His threats continued.

This is clearly a case in which the nurturing of Connie by her husband was painfully absent. Although their marriage had other, positive aspects, Connie felt stifled, as if there were "no hope" for her becoming more of who she really is—of self-actualizing. The status quo continued.

In some cases, the help of a skilled therapist can resolve certain issues, but sometimes all the therapeutic skill in the world is ineffective. For the most part, I've observed many couples effectively using the *Tools* to resolve difficult problems by themselves; these are the couples who truly desire to change and grow. And they are almost always the ones who are secure enough to nurture their partner's growth.

▣ TOOL #1

UNDERPINNINGS:
Six Qualities to Help Love Thrive

The following are brief summaries of each quality:

1. COMMITMENT ("No Exit" Decision)
Both partners are committed to remain in the relationship. No talk of separation, breakup, divorce, assault or addictions that numb either partner from being "present" (e.g., alcohol, drugs), no "breakdowns," suicide threats, etc.

2. SAFETY
Feeling that both partners can relax, be comfortable, be honest and be their "real selves" with the other. No fear of emotional or physical harm, no throwing, hitting, bodily or property damage; no psychological fear of annihilation or of becoming "invisible" to the partner.

3. TRUST
Each person specifies things they can honestly promise to *do* or *not do* based on the partner's requests. Written agreements are often helpful (both partners have a copy). When you keep

your word and do what you promised, Trust develops. (Make sure never to promise to do something that in good faith you know you cannot do—or are not ready to do.) It is far more important that your partner trusts you to tell the *truth*, rather than simply "giving in" to what *they want*.

4. OPEN COMMUNICATION
Communication has two basic parts:

• **Self-Disclosure**—sending clear, honest, non-manipulative messages. Primarily statements about yourself, how you feel, requests you have, etc. (e.g., "I feel....I need....I want to....")
• **Active Listening** (also known as **Mirroring**): the accurate summarizing and repeating back what the other person has said from *his/her* point of view (with no "contamination" of your own opinions. Attempts to **Mirror** must be repeated until the partner is satisfied that you *heard* them accurately. **Note:** This has *nothing* to do with agreement, validity or your advice. It is only *an accurate understanding* of what the other person said.

5. EMPATHY/KNOWLEDGE
Insight and knowledge about the partner's fears, desires, pain, motivation, childhood trauma, "life script," adult goals, frustrations, and sources of pleasure and satisfaction. This includes not only a deep understanding of the partner's temperament, personality type, primary needs and values, but also a willingness to honor and support these.

6. NURTURING
One's ability to assist the other in becoming *more of who he/she really is*, to *self-actualize*, and to use more of his/her potential

(talents, intelligence, aptitude) for becoming more fully himself/herself. (Not to simply manipulate the partner into becoming more of what *you want* them to be.) Nurturing is much easier when you have high self-esteem, confidence in your own abilities and achievements, and a sense of empowerment. (Feeling insecure, threatened or jealous makes this very difficult.)

NOTE:

Sometimes individuals need to solve their own issues before they are capable of nurturing a partner.

* * *

INSTRUCTIONS FOR TOOL #1:

1) To benefit most from working with this Tool, begin by planning one hour of quiet, uninterrupted time with your partner. Decide who will go first with rating the partner on items 1, 3 and 5. (The other person will go first when rating the partner on items 2, 4 and 6.)

2) The goal is to rate your partner (and eventually yourself) on a scale of 0 to 10. Zero indicates a complete absence of this condition, with a 10 indicating that this trait is present in full force, all the time.

* * *

<u>NOTE:</u> For couples who *wish to do a second process*, at a separate time, rate yourself on the same 0 to 10 scale. This is your own perception of your personal ability to create and provide this condition for your partner. Discuss the differences between your partner's and your own ratings *at a later date.*

PERSON A _____
(name)

	RATING of 0 – 10 for **PARTNER**	RATING of 0 – 10 for **SELF**
Quality #1 **Commitment**	_____	_____
Quality #2 **Safety**	_____	_____
Quality #3 **Trust**	_____	_____
Quality #4 **Open Communication**	_____	_____
Quality #5 **Empathy/Knowledge**	_____	_____
Quality #6 **Nurturing**	_____	_____

RATING SCALE:

0 = absence of quality

1-4 = lesser degrees of presence

5 = moderate presence of quality

6-9 = greater degree of presence

10 = consistent presence of quality

PERSONAL NOTES PAGE:

Record your indivdual thoughts, reactions, comments, and questions below.

PERSON B _____
          (name)

	RATING of 0 – 10 for **PARTNER**	RATING of 0 – 10 for **SELF**
Quality #1 **Commitment**	_____	_____
Quality #2 **Safety**	_____	_____
Quality #3 **Trust**	_____	_____
Quality #4 **Open Communication**	_____	_____
Quality #5 **Empathy/Knowledge**	_____	_____
Quality #6 **Nurturing**	_____	_____

RATING SCALE:

0   = **absence of quality**

1-4 = **lesser degrees of presence**

5   = **moderate presence of quality**

6-9 = **greater degree of presence**

10   = **consistent presence of quality**

PERSONAL NOTES PAGE:

Record your indivdual thoughts, reactions, comments, and questions below.

THE REAL VALUE OF THIS TOOL

The most impotant aspect of this excercise is to learn about yourself and your partner. Discuss each quality *in depth* so that you have a better understanding of your mate's needs, feelings, desires and expectations.

It is strategically important to assess the *actual state* of your relationship. Make an effort to discover which of these six qualities are *weakest* and which are *strongest* in your relationship. Try to work out any plans, promises or new behaviors that might enhance these qualities for each of you.

2

LOVE, LIKING AND LUST:
What Shape Is Your Triangle?

Since the early years I spent developing this model, I've become increasingly aware that *all three sides* of this triangle are desirable ingredients for a fully functional and successful love relationship. However, the majority of couples have a lopsided "triangle" in which at least one component—or maybe two—is undeveloped or dormant in the relationship.

This is only a framework for deciphering the general weaknesses and strengths of your relationship. Perhaps *Tool #2* can help you as a couple to make plans or agreements to improve the quality and spirit of your togetherness.

Some couples may need to do nothing more than set aside *time* to do more things together (e.g., play tennis, play cards, take a bicycle ride, have a dinner date without the children, see a good movie). They may have forgotten *why* they originally enjoyed each other's company—why they *Liked* being together.

In other cases, the *Lust* may have "dribbled away" or simply shut down; in some cases, it was never there at all. Many couples simply become so busy, exhausted and worn down from the demands of daily living that the "chemistry" (i.e., the eroticism, the animal desire for sexual contact) collapses into a need for sleep.

Quite a few couples "function effectively" with *Lust* being completely dormant. The price for this is that the deeper physical/emotional bonding can be gravely weakened. The triangle becomes much more lopsided.

For most couples it's *not* necessary to seek formal sex therapy, but rather to **set aside time and energy** for each other; this cannot be successful if one or both of you are dead tired. Just half an hour set aside for hugging and kissing (and who knows what else) might have wonderful results. Just having the leisure time and energy could make all the difference.

In some relationships the deep *Love* connection of being wholly committed could be stifled, damaged or never really developed. I've known many couples who are not totally committed to their partner's highest good and well being. This means valuing the other person as much as you value yourself.

When this kind of *Love* is present, you see the partner as a "precious human treasure": someone you want to encourage, build up and assist in becoming all they can be. The very nature of committed love is unselfish and giving from the heart.

When *Love* is missing, the relationship can feel hollow and without substance. The couple may have great sex, lots of excitement and friends (mostly for distraction); they may enjoy many activities, common values, travel and a beautiful home—but when *Love* is missing, the "triangle" can get flat. There is only the bonding between *Liking* and *Lust*, with no *Love* to fill it out.

Over four decades of counseling, I've come to the conclusion that a significant number of couples have at least one side of their triangle essentially weak or missing, and that's okay. They have no desire to upset the convenience of their lifestyle or alter the status quo.

Although the happiest and most personally satisfied couples

appear to have all three basic ingredients (or at least the awareness and motivation to "flesh them out"), there are exceptions.

I feel compelled to explain a few of these exceptions, lest you, my reader, get the erroneous impression that these three variables are *absolutely necessary for a functional relationship*. They're *not*, and here's *why*.

LOVE, LIKING AND LUST

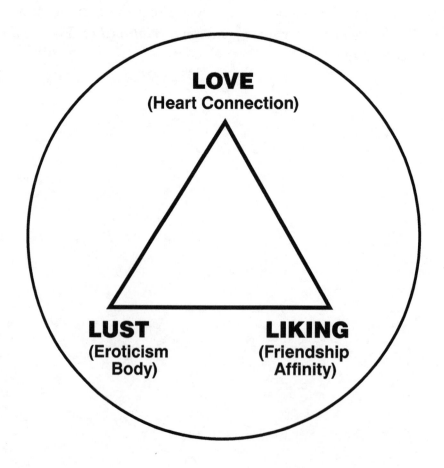

WHEN *LOVE* IS MISSING

First, when **Love**, the deep heart connection, *is missing*, a couple can still function on the aspects of *Lust* and *Liking* that are present.

I'm reminded of a couple who sought my counseling because Cynthia, the wife, demanded it. Her husband, Brian, was a scientist; he appeared cold and aloof and described himself as a "hard-nosed, no-nonsense atheist." Cynthia was frazzled, emotional and a "good Mormon." At the time of their marriage (five years earlier) he had promised to "look into becoming a Mormon." She was impressed by his intelligence and ability to "get things done."

Cynthia had continually hounded Brian about studying *The Book of Mormon*, with the result that he became more reclusive and "dug in his heels" regarding atheism. Fighting and arguments between them that formerly erupted from time to time had recently intensified, especially during the past two years, since the birth of their daughter, whom they both cherished.

Both admitted that the "once-felt love" between them had died (or perhaps was never present). They had many other good reasons and motives for marrying. And now the biggest reason of all for staying together was their beloved daughter, whom they wanted to have a "loving, stable home environment." Their functional sex life and the fact that his high salary allowed her not to work outside the home—plus her excellence as a housekeeper and cook—kept them together.

Without deep Love, the heartfelt connection was essentially missing, but their marriage remained intact with their two-sided dynamic.

They had little desire to change anything in their relationship, though they did agree "never to discuss religion again." This arrangement allowed them the convenience of continuing as a "functional" family.

Here's another example of a married couple (early 30s, no children) who had the *Love* portion of their triangle missing. Both Marsha and Roger were highly paid corporate executives who enjoyed their work. They had agreed never to "burden" themselves with children and appeared highly compatible from the outside. They were essentially male and female versions of the same lifestyle, interests, hobbies, and family background. In addition, they enjoyed an excellent sex life.

One autumn day Marsha's company offered her a fabulous position overseas. It would double her already high salary and the company would pay all moving expenses, but she would have to live in Germany. At first, she seemed distraught over the decision, but then realized she would "love the adventure of Europe."

Roger could make no such move. His company existed only in the United States, and he was not willing to "quit and start over." Within two weeks, their minds were made up, and they were in complete agreement.

No great pain or drama was involved. They filed for divorce the following week. As she packed for the move, Marsha felt increasingly excited about living in Europe; Roger was busy looking for "a new roommate." They parted as "the best of friends."

The deep *Love* and heartfelt connection that might have caused them to put their marriage first was simply missing.

WHEN *LIKING* IS MISSING

In another series of cases, I remember couples with whom the *Liking* element—being "best friends"—was the missing one. Allison and Tony, a dynamic young couple who had lived together for five years, were "turning 30 this summer and considering marriage." They came to see me because they had "nothing in common" and thought they might need counseling.

As I dug deeper into their relationship, I quickly discovered how profoundly they loved one another. They were deeply bonded and had made many sacrifices for one another. For example, when Tony shattered his left leg surfing, she nursed him and took over most of his daily chores for many months. He had a well-paid sales career (to which he was able to return), but eventually the medical benefits ran out. Allison was able to cope with all of his medical and caregiving needs and expenses, in addition to keeping her own career as a tax accountant functioning efficiently.

When "time allowed," they both reported a "pretty good sex life" with lots of closeness and touching.

But the "nothing in common" issue was a significant problem. He described himself as a high-energy, high-performing salesman whose main hobby was "serious surfing" every chance he got, with guitar playing a close second.

Allison could not have been more different: an introvert, she was a successful tax accountant who loved numbers and described herself as "very business-minded." Her hobbies included reading serious history and biographies. She was "afraid of the water," and the very idea of surfing made her nervous. Her lack of interest in music was in strong contrast with Tony's obsessiveness about learning to play the guitar and listening to small local bands and guitarists that she found "boring and unprofessional."

This was the flavor of their many, many differences. They didn't *Like* what their partner was interested in and were not good run-around pals. Their friendship was often strained—and sometimes ruptured—by their conflicting interests and values. This was the reason they had sought my counsel.

I mirrored back to them what they had communicated to me about their deep loyalty and commitment to one another, with all the examples of serious sacrifices they had made for one another (including her ability to finish her accounting degree and licensing because of his financial support, and his dependence on her after his surfing accident). Their *Love* was genuine and strong, and their "chemistry" for sex had continued throughout their five years together.

I asked if they could possibly have one "date" per week that they **both Liked** and enjoyed. The only two activities they could agree upon were "going out to dinner" and "good movies." With their busy careers, could they be happy with "one date a week," time reserved just for one another?

They considered this seriously and mutually came to understand that "the reality of breaking up" would be so devastating that living with their incompatible "likes and dislikes" was a small price to pay.

Continuing to enjoy their strong *Love* and commitment, they began a weekly exercise (which I designed for them) to underline and deepen the aspects of their relationship that were already fulfilling.

This helped them enormously. They found new ways to support and encourage each other's interests. Their weekly "date" began with them taking turns initiating and planning how they would spend this time together—usually movie tickets and/or restaurant reservations. Occasionally they became "creative." One summer weekend, when it was "her turn," Allison planned a delicious picnic lunch at the beach, followed by an outdoor band concert (with lots of guitars).

About two years later they sent me an invitation to their wedding.

WHEN *LUST* IS MISSING

Another extreme exception to the balanced relationship depicted by the equilateral triangle is the one in which the *Lust* element is *missing*, repressed, or just vaguely absent. Again, the effect is to basically deflate the triangle into an open two-sided figure that appears unstable.

The very nature of *Lust* (eroticism, the yearning for tactile/sensual connection) is by definition physical. In rare cases, there may be hormonal deficiencies or other bodily ailments that can kill sexual desire, but, in general, the dynamics are emotionally based.

The following two cases are exceptions to the general rule that most couples can work out their own dilemmas by seriously using some of the ten *Tools* presented in this book. These examples are both of couples who felt they needed "outside, professional help" to resolve the issues that were troubling them.

One couple, Carol and Walter, had "struggled for years" with continual arguing, debating and correcting one another's opinions—conflicts that often erupted into vicious fighting. They had both "turned 50 in the last two years," and both of their sons were now away at college, which seemed to facilitate their fighting becoming more open and vocal.

The early years of their marriage had been exceptionally strained. Walter suffered a major business bankruptcy, for which Carol had little empathy. She suffered greatly from two excruciating childbirth experiences, during which he displayed little or no compassion for her.

Their "short-lived romance" had become a life of drudgery and strife. The marriage felt like a hollow, empty routine of competitive debating and arguing about their conflicting views and values. In their words, "Any *Love* we may once have had . . . *died*."

They no longer had any physical attraction for one another. She commented loudly that "masturbation was by far preferable" to being with him. He agreed, explaining that it was way too difficult to "hug a porcupine." Their fights continued.

Both were relieved that their two sons were "living away, at college" not exposed to their constant bickering. They claimed they had "nothing in common" and essentially didn't *Like* one another. They had no friends in common and no mutual interests or activities.

I tried in many ways, as a marriage counselor, to see if their relationship could be revived. Why did they *marry* each other to begin with? What were their hopes and dreams for a family? Their two sons had apparently turned out to be "great guys," and Walter's now successful business provided them with a comfortable lifestyle.

I realized as our talks continued that they were actually looking for *permission to get divorced*. They wanted a "professional opinion" that their marriage had truly died.

So I offered the "option of a peaceful, friendly divorce." They could sell their big house, and both live in smaller condos or homes with a second bedroom for the boys' visits. They both smiled for the first time and appeared to breathe a sigh of relief. This was the first time, in all of our sessions, that there was any direct eye contact between them. A new spirit of collaboration was trying to emerge.

They happily and successfully divorced.

Another "exceptional" case in which the *Lust* was *absent* was that of Willa and Karl, a young, seemingly happy couple (late 20s, married four years, no children, and no plans ever to have children). I was rather perplexed in our first session as to why they had made an appointment with me.

As our first interview progressed, I realized they had never consummated their marriage. They were both still "virgins" in the marriage. They seemed eager to explain their mutual traumas and why there was a complete absence of sexual interest. *Lust* had *never existed* for either of them in any relationship.

Karl had been traumatized—sexually and emotionally— by his own mother. She insisted on incest with him as a young boy (ages 9 to 13). At 13, he went to live with an aunt and uncle after his mother was arrested for theft related to her drug addiction.

He was so completely turned off to *anything* sexual, he subconsciously "closed the door" to ever wanting, or even thinking about, any form of sexual activity. The very idea made him feel sick to his stomach.

This was perfectly okay with his sweet wife, for she too felt "complete revulsion" around anything sexual. She reported her "stomach turning" at the thought of penetration or intercourse. The conversation was on thin ice already, and I didn't want to push her for details. However, she was anxious to "get it out" and let me know "the truth."

She had been gang raped as a 17-year-old virgin. While walking home from her high school cheerleading practice on a warm autumn evening, she suddenly found herself surrounded by "three good-looking boys." They were teasing her, flirting and asking her to "get it on" because she was "so pretty."

Beginning to feel afraid, she announced to the boys that she was going to "jog home." They vehemently protested, grabbed her by both arms, still flirting, and forcefully escorted her into a thicket of bushes and trees. One by one, they commenced to rape her, holding her mouth shut with their hands, then a bandana, threatening to "really hurt" her if she "didn't shut up."

Following the triple rape, the boys quickly ran away and left her lying helpless in the bushes. After a while, she found her Bermuda shorts and hobbled home. She chose not to tell her parents about the "disaster" she had experienced, fearing the worst consequences. Her dad had a horrible temper; he would most likely go after the boys and "try to kill them." He would make sure she had "no more cheerleading" in her senior year.

The three boys were obviously older (probably 19 or 20) and not from her school district. She vowed "not to tell anyone and never, ever to allow the humiliation and violence of sex" to have any part in her life.

So there we had it—the perfect match. Neither of the partners wanted anything to do with *Lust.* Their unspoken agreement to "never try anything sexual" was a welcome relief for them both, and it built a strong bond of trust between them.

They had a strong *Love* and high degree of *Liking* for each other. Also, they were markedly compatible in their religious and political beliefs, their hobbies and interests, goals for travel and vacations, plus many other variables.

I realized Willa and Karl were actually asking me, as a "marriage counselor," if their marriage was legitimate. Was it morally and spiritually okay not to ever have sex? To never consummate their marriage? To have no children?

I assured them that *every* couple has the *perfect right to construct their own unique marriage,* in whatever way the two of them desire. It was *their business*, and no one else's.

Yes, of course their marriage was legitimate, I said. In fact, they were "happier and more bonded than many other couples." Their deepest emotional needs and fears were being met by the partner. Furthermore, they were satisfied and deeply happy with their "two-sided" dynamic. I explained to them what it meant to be the "successful exception."

⊡ TOOL #2

LOVE, LIKING AND LUST:
What Shape Is Your Triangle?

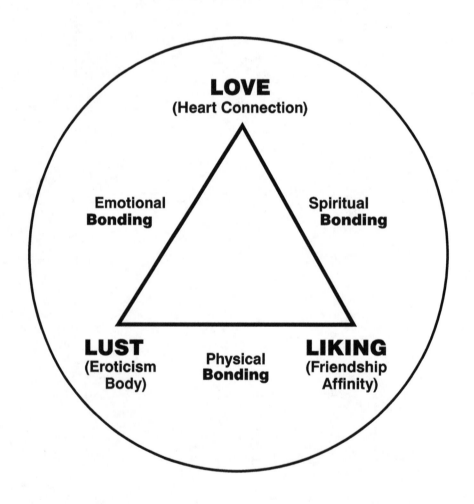

The Love, Liking and Lust triangle provides a paradigm, a model, for couples to evaluate and discuss the various aspects of their relationship. Most couples can use *Tool #2* to make their own decisions and plans for enrichment, without the help of a professional counselor or sex therapist.

Even if one arm of the triangle is completely missing, a couple may still have a viable relationship, with excellent communication however limited.

1) **Please use *Tool #2* for your own personal and private discussion. Analyze the three components as objectively as you can with your partner.**

2) **Together, map out your own desires and plans as a couple, to *create your own triangle* the way you want it to be. This can be an exciting and powerful journey into greater intimacy. It is also a powerful excercise for uncovering your partner's feelings and true perceptions**

3

LOVE STYLES:
Different Ways of Giving Love

When I first read Gary Chapman's book *The 5 Love Languages,* I was impressed by its simplicity as well as its potential for helping couples. These five categories provided a framework for people to communicate what they valued and needed from their partner in order to feel truly loved.

I call my version of this *Tool (#3) LOVE STYLES: Different Ways of Giving Love.* One of the shortest and most precisely focused of the *Tools* in this book, it can offer couples great clarity about *how* and *what* an individual needs to feel loved and valued by the partner.

There are no doubt additional categories of behaviors, traditions and attitudes that cause a person to feel cherished. However, these five represent types of behavior that are most commonly demonstrated (or complained about) among committed couples.

So why not try to specify precisely what styles you and your partner most desire from each other? Understanding this can trigger new actions and a sensitivity to the partner's needs that were previously unconscious. These are among the *Tools* that make romantic love expand and thrive.

KNOWING WHAT YOU NEED

In the process of further developing this *Tool*, I remembered with pleasure a couple in their late 30s whom my husband and I met on vacation. The four of us got talking, and when they discovered I was a marriage counselor they inquired about the deeper things that could help them feel closer. I'll call them Barbara and Jim. They were an interesting pair who obviously loved one another. They wanted this cruise to be "romantic," a "real boost" for their marriage and communication.

I quickly sketched out on a sheet of paper the five "love languages," explained each briefly and repeated the list and descriptions on a second page. I asked them not to discuss anything on the page prior to rating the items. Once they had both completed the ratings, they could compare their number one through number five scores. When they did this, they discovered a completely new idea of who their partner was.

In a later conversation Barbara said her number one (most important) way of feeling loved was through Gifts, while Jim's number one was Words. Both seemed surprised by the other's answers.

Barbara continued to explain that her family (parents and two sisters) focus was on celebrations of gift giving. For them, this was the ultimate form of love; they offered each other special items that marked not only birthdays, anniversaries, holidays, childbirth and christenings but also illnesses and accidents. Gifts apparently constituted her family's way of measuring care and devotion.

One of Barbara's "silent" complaints about Jim (which she didn't want to tell him directly for fear of "hurting his feelings") was that he "talked a lot about things." In fact, she felt he talked too much and "never came through" with *real* gifts.

In a separate conversation with Jim, I got the strong impression that he enjoyed "talking things over" with Barbara. He was a successful public speaker who loved sharing ideas, telling stories and explaining his opinions. His ability to explain things was exceptional, and he never fully understood Barbara's tendency to withdraw from conversations.

Later that week, when the four of us met up again, it was apparent that Barbara and Jim's newfound awareness of each other's "Love Languages" had already brought about significant changes in their relationship.

Jim was happy to show off the new bracelet he had bought for Barbara to commemorate their "romantic vacation." While Barbara truly loved the bracelet, she was even more excited to explain how the talks she and Jim had had about their "differences" and "priorities" had triggered in both of them a new determination to please each other by *doing what each of them personally desired* (rather than projecting onto the partner their own values).

Barbara later commented, when I was sitting alone with her, how lucky she felt to have Jim be so "open and willing to discuss everything" rather than being quiet and shut down the way a lot of their friends were. Their romance was blossoming before my eyes, and the cruise gave a "tremendous boost" to their marriage.

ALL ABOUT FOOTBALL AND BEING PHYSICAL

I'll describe one more example of how this particular "Love Languages" *Tool* provided crucial help in a much more serious case. In this instance, intervention with depth counseling was imperative.

Janet, a petite and composed math teacher at a private high school, was in her early 40s, unmarried, and childless (by choice). She sought my help about her live-in relationship with Herb. The pair had been committed lovers, best friends, travel companions and "good roommates" for over 15 years. Both enjoyed their relationship in its current form.

Neither desired a formal marriage, neither wanted children, neither liked the idea of being "bound by contracts." Janet was a loyal, dutiful and somewhat introverted "private" person. She especially enjoyed quiet time and long casual visits with dear friends.

Herb, however, had little desire or appreciation for this style of living. His main interest was more physical, expressed by a desire to "move, play sports, have sex and get massages" for his sore muscles. Janet had always known he was "a real jock," and he was perfectly suited for his career as head football coach at the local high school.

His preference for "physical pleasure" had intensified over the past couple of years and now had begun to trouble Janet. Although she enjoyed their great lovemaking, she had recently become exasperated over his desire for "constant sex." There was no time to "just relax, go places as a couple, take some romantic trips together." She resented the fact that every time they went away, it was "always for some football game."

Janet sincerely loved Herb, but was increasingly alienated by his "super jock" lifestyle. His constant focus on sports, coaching and games had finally "taken its toll," and she felt there was no room for her in his life.

When Herb first came in to see me, at Janet's insistence, he was polite but confessed his frustration and irritation with her for forcing him "to spend this much time and money on just talking!" He declared his love for her and asked to "be excused."

I explained that this type of counseling was always voluntary (with no force involved), but for couples who wanted to remain together it was vital to *learn each other's love styles.*

Herb looked perplexed.

I finally managed to grab his attention by commenting that if he gave all his best instructions and coaching plays to his team in Chinese, *no one* would understand. The language he'd chosen for such communication was the wrong one; it was imperative that he speak in English, which was the language his players understood and needed him to use if his coaching was to be effective.

I explained that relationships are much the same. In order for both people to feel loved, it's vital that each partner deliver the message in the Language the other needs and desires.

I gave them both this five-question *Tool*, explained that they had four minutes to fill it out separately. When the time was up I retrieved their surveys and began reading the results aloud. To no one's surprise, their least important (number five) behaviors had to do with "Gifts."

I commented on how compatible they were with what didn't matter very much. They chuckled on learning that their next-to-least important (number four) categories were also identical: "Acts of Service."

Next up was their most important category (number one), and these were quite the opposite. It came as no surprise that Herb's most valued "Love Language" was *Touch*. He explained that this was his first choice because it included "kissing, having sex, playing sports, getting massages, etc." He felt this was the "main reason for any couple to live together. . . . It's so obvious!"

At this point I explained that Janet's top priority (number one) was *Quality Time* together. What caused her to feel truly loved was spending "alone time together." She longed to take little romantic trips, lie in bed together talking, take coffee breaks together after school, or just sit together reading.

Herb expressed surprise at Janet's ranking Touch as number

three, but she seemed to have expected that Touch would be his number one priority. I pointed out that they also shared a common "Love Language," with Words being their common number two ranking. Both enjoyed talking and had no trouble with verbal communication.

It finally dawned on Herb that he had been speaking to Janet "in Chinese."

Although she gained much enjoyment from their sex life, what made her feel really loved was the *"alone time"* with him.

She again emphasized how much she needed "little day trips; short, romantic vacations that didn't involve football . . . just little breaks from work to talk and be together."

Herb responded with amazement and delight. It was clear that he sincerely wanted Janet to be happy.

This felt like the perfect moment to introduce the importance of *"re-entry" time*. When a couple first "connects" (i.e., gets back together, in person)—usually at the end of the work day—the first ten minutes set the tone for the remainder of the day.

This has proved to be a crucial ten minutes for most couples (especially those who work). I advised them to "set aside all other concerns, just for this initial ten minutes (i.e., *not* to discuss work problems or personal frustrations, *not* to open the mail, *not* to check cell phones, *not* to turn on the TV or computer—but simply to "be present" for their partner).

This ten-minute period (sometimes reduced to only five minutes) allows the couple to "reconnect" through having a loving, thoughtful conversation, perhaps accompanied by a glass of wine or cup of tea. It provides the space to non-verbally say, "I care about you and your day; you're worth my time."

Herb appeared flabbergasted that he had never thought of doing such a thing. At first, he stumbled over his words, apologizing to Janet, then directly asked her if this "re-entry time" was something she really wanted. Was this actually important to her?

With tears streaming down her cheeks, she answered quietly, "Yes. It's because I love you, Herb. I need your *time* to show me your love is sincere."

Again Herb seemed surprised but he managed this time to stay with the conversation. "Janet, you must know how much I love you. . . I've been loyal and devoted to you for 15 years! There could never be anyone else. I'm happy to give you my *time*, if that's what you need to feel really loved."

Herb later followed up on his clear intentions to "take more long walks, go to the beach together, have "mini-dates," as he called them. He also wanted to plan an annual summer trip just for the two of them.

Since their sensual/sexual life was already satisfying for both of them, Herb didn't have any requests for change in Janet. All was well.

After only one "formal therapy" session and the use of one simple *Tool*, Herb suddenly believed in "therapy" and apologized for his previous negativity.

⊡ TOOL #3

LOVE STYLES:
Different Ways of Giving Love

It is useful to study the concepts in Gary Chapman's book, *The 5 Love Languages* and assess your true feelings before making your *Priority Ratings:*

— Gifts / Physical Mementos

— Touch / Holding

— Acts of Service / Help

— Quality Time

— Words / Conversation

The objective of this *Tool* is to discover two basic things:

1) What makes *you* feel truly loved and cheriched by your partner.

2) What behaviors make your *partner* feel truly loved and cherished by you.

INSTRUCTIONS FOR TOOL #3:
(LOVE STYLES: *Different Ways of Giving Love*)

PART I DIRECTIONS:

Use the following 2 forms for Person A and Person B to record your ratings:

Rank the following 5 groups of behaviors based on what causes *you* to feel loved by your partner.

(#1 is your most important;
#5 is least important to you.)

PART II DIRECTIONS:

1) After you have completed your ratings, fully explain to your partner why you chose #1 as your top priority. Listen carefully to your partner's explanation for his/her #1 choice.

2) Both of you explain why you put the item you did as #5 (your lowest priority). Take turns by practicing "Active Listening" to be certain you've heard the partner's intended message.

3) Continue discussion of your Ranking of all 5 groups, until your partner has a clear picture of what causes you to feel loved and cherished and vice versa.

PERSON A _____
(name)

_____ **Gifts/Physical Mementos:** Material items, receiving things you want: surprise presents, items that mark "special occasions" (e.g., birthdays, anniversaries).

_____ **Touch/Holding** Hand-holding, hugs, massage, physical contact, lovemaking, casual affection, ranging from kisses to pats on the back.

_____ **Acts of Service/Help:** Favors, good will gestures, help with chores, offering assistance in meeting their goals, being "present" to do whatever needs to be done.

_____ **Quality Time:** Dates, vacations, time spent alone as a couple, prioritizing work and activities so that you have time for shared experiences as a romantic pair.

_____ **Words/Conversation:** Terms of endearment, saying "sweet nothings, personal conversation, desire to "talk things over," verbal communication that implies: "you're worth my time."

PERSONAL NOTES PAGE:

Record your indivdual thoughts, reactions, comments, and questions below.

PERSON B _____
　　　　　(name)

_____ **Gifts/Physical Mementos:** Material items, receiving things you want: surprise presents, items that mark "special occasions" (e.g., birthdays, anniversaries).

_____ **Touch/Holding** Hand-holding, hugs, massage, physical contact, lovemaking, casual affection, ranging from kisses to pats on the back.

_____ **Acts of Service/Help:** Favors, good will gestures, help with chores, offering assistance in meeting their goals, being "present" to do whatever needs to be done.

_____ **Quality Time:** Dates, vacations, time spent alone as a couple, prioritizing work and activities so that you have time for shared experiences as a romantic pair.

_____ **Words/Conversation:** Terms of endearment, saying "sweet nothings, personal conversation, desire to "talk things over," verbal communication that implies: "you're worth my time."

PERSONAL NOTES PAGE:

Record your indivdual thoughts, reactions, comments, and questions below.

4

INTIMACY RATING:
How Do You Score?

Of the ten *Tools* presented in this book, the *Intimacy Rating* has proved the most popular and often the most helpful for couples in committed relationships.

This *Tool* takes the longest to complete. If the Discussion Instructions are followed as suggested, your "hourly sessions" might extend over a period of five to seven weeks. Some couples enjoy comparing their scores, talking briefly about a few differences and moving on without the in-depth discussion. Still others prefer to talk about each of the 50 statements in depth.

This kind of in-depth discussion should be limited to one hour per week (or, in some cases, to several 15-minute or 30-minute sessions, totaling no more than one hour per week). The intensity of this kind of conversation can become overwhelming for some individuals. The best choice is usually to pace yourselves. Take the survey, get your ratings, compare them with your partner's, and see where the discussion leads you.

At the beginning of your first session, it might be a good idea to set a timer for 15 minutes. If you feel comfortable going on with the conversation when the timer goes off, give yourself another 15 minutes. When that second period is up, if you still feel positive about continuing, set the timer for 30 minutes and finish your weekly allotment of one hour—when that time runs out.

BEING A "WINNER"

One couple that I knew socially (who were not my therapy clients) insisted on taking the survey after hearing about it from friends. I'll call them Pete and MarySue.

Pete flew into a rage when he added up his score (about 42 percent and saw that MarySue's was also quite low, at 46 percent.

"How could this be?" Pete fumed as he defended his "twenty-some years of marriage" as basically "stable" and "functional."

MarySue agreed: they had a highly functional relationship, one without much intimacy. She admitted that she longed for "more depth" and personal caring between her and Pete. But two young teenage children, two careers, one serious car accident, death of a parent on both sides, and "life in general" had taken a toll on the marriage and deepened the "rut" they were in.

Pete, who was used to being an "All-time Winner," had never scored as low as 42 percent on anything in his life. "Not even in high school!" MarySue had less ego involved in the survey and painfully admitted that about 46 percent was an accurate "ballpark figure for how much intimacy was lacking" in their marriage.

They were smart enough to begin strategizing about ways to "increase romance" in their lives. I learned later, from mutual friends, (clients of mine who had passed along my *Intimacy Survey* to them) that they began having weekly dates, with "mini-dates" in between. Pete, especially, was determined to remain a "winner."

The result, not surprisingly, was that they became more affectionate with one another (and also with their teenage children). Trust and compassion grew as they discussed all fifty statements. *Tool #4* was a perfect "wake-up call" for them.

PRESSURE FOR PREGNANCY

Another potent example of how the *Intimacy Rating* helped a couple in distress was the case of Beth and Greg. They were a high-powered double-income pair with no children.

Beth was growing tired of her highly demanding executive position and felt desperate to have a baby. Four attempts at artificial insemination had failed, and now she was demanding expensive in-vitro fertilization. Greg was worn out and admitted he was "tired of it all."

The once-great intimacy they had shared had now drained out of their marriage. Both appeared "threadbare" and alienated from the other. Beth, weeping, said she felt like a failure, while Greg said he had been reduced to "nothing but a sperm machine." Their former deep intimacy seemed to have evaporated.

They had difficulty making direct eye contact with each other. I suggested that we back up a bit, put the baby issue on hold, and first address the problems in their marriage. They agreed to this approach.

To start, I requested that they take the *Intimacy Rating* separately from one another and bring me their scores, which they did. Both were in the 55-60 percent range; each felt alienated and disconnected from the other.

During the following few weeks they agreed to discuss the 50 items in depth during 15-minute sessions, (never exceeding a total of one hour per week). Over a period of five weeks, they discovered a new appreciation for each other. The deeper empathy and sense of relief that evolved between them encouraged a rebirth of their romantic love.

Beth finally realized that much of the pressure she felt to get pregnant came from her four closest girl friends (three of whom had infants and the fourth was pregnant). She herself wasn't even sure she wanted children. Suddenly, the prospect of being an "aunt" to her friends' little ones felt like a relief.

Greg reported that he hadn't seen Beth this happy in the past two years. Her relaxed attitude, he said, created the space for him to fall back in love with her. He admitted that he had always felt ambivalent about parenthood. Willing to "go either way," he wanted, above all, to see Beth happy.

The overwhelming relief that came with Beth's discovery that she might not even want parenthood allowed her to recognize that her career still meant a lot to her, even though she didn't feel obligated to take every advancement opportunity her company offered.

She reveled in being in love again with Greg, whom she saw as a "great husband." All this added up to both of them experiencing a huge sense of freedom.

They agreed to pursue their respective careers in a relaxed way, take more vacations and make love more often (for pleasure, not pregnancy). Obviously, the *Intimacy Rating* triggered the right kind of soul-searching and problem solving that this couple desperately needed.

CHILDREN IN SECOND MARRIAGES

An unusual couple, Angie, 68 and Sam, 72, came to see me professionally, after dating for two years, because they felt something was "amiss" in their relationship but couldn't figure out what the problem was.

They made a charming, handsome couple—both highly educated, both widowed for a number of years, both lonely and wanting a "solid" relationship. What could possibly be the problem? Why seek advice from a marriage counselor?

They spoke freely and easily about how they were introduced, how much they enjoyed each other's company and a number of common interests they had. The only area of distress appeared to be their children. Angie had raised "two wonderful kids," and Sam had "three great guys," all following in his footsteps in the insurance business. Sam had single-handedly built a thriving insurance agency, in which all three sons were extremely successful.

Still, this "mysterious" discomfort hung over them.

"Just for fun," I invited them to take the *Intimacy Rating* survey. Both were open to this and eager to know their scores.

The following week Sam presented his 94 percent, while Angie was clearly proud of her 92 percent. These were their scores "in private," when none of their five children were around. They agreed that their scores would be "much lower" if they took the survey as a measure of behavior when the kids were a consideration.

As I questioned them further, they agreed that all five kids seemed seriously threatened by their romance. One of Sam's sons questioned the future of their agency "with Angie in the picture." Angie's younger daughter seemed to mistrust Sam. "He's probably just after your money," she told her mom.

Bingo! Here we had two mature people falling in love, with significant estates and inheritances for their children, feeling their strong relationship with each other was being undermined by their children's fear. The issue on the children's minds, evidently, was: If a legal marriage were to take place between Angie and Sam, would their kids be at risk for losing their inheritance?

All five children had expressed some form of disapproval of Angie and Sam's relationship, questioning *why* the other person was so interested in their parent.

Listening closely, having had previous experience with many "inheritance cases," I presented what I thought might be the source of the concern and discontent for the children on both sides.

Angie and Sam took my comments lightly and chuckled as they explained to me that they'd already discussed this issue. More questioning from me revealed that, although the couple had indeed "covered these points" together, they had never discussed the issue with their respective children. Both had Living Trusts, Wills, Powers of Attorney and other appropriate documents, and each had already insured that their own children would directly inherit their personal estate.

Despite the care Sam and Angie had taken to "cover all these points" together, they had left out one vital element: they had *never made their arrangements clear to their children.*

I encouraged them to immediately arrange meetings with their respective children and lay out in detail how their Living Trusts and other legal instruments worked. Since all the legal work had been done to insure each parent's estate would go to his/her children, there could be no threat from any potential marriage.

Following their respective family meetings, all five children "came around." Their relief about their parents' arrangement to protect their offspring's legacies was reflected in the comments some of them began making about marriage. Teasing their parents about setting "a wedding date," they jokingly encouraged the couple to "become legitimate" for the "sake of their grandkids."

Angie and Sam's happiness blossomed, now that the one negative aspect of their romance—their children's uneasiness about it—had disappeared. They began discussing "real marriage" as a way to live their "92 percent and 94 percent intimacy" full time.

One by one, all five children became supportive and grateful for their parents' "new-found love."

As a couple, Sam and Angie never really needed the *Intimacy Rating,* per se, but *Tool #4* allowed them to see how a "double standard" had developed when their children became involved. They were smart enough to quickly resolve the situation through open and frank discussion with each child and showing all of them the legal documents related to their inheritance.

* * *

Follow the directions for *Tool #4* on the two forms that follow and see what you discover.

Getting your "Intimacy Rating," then seeing which Percentage-Rating Group you are in can be quite informative.

Using the suggestions in the "Discussion for Couples" section at the end of *Tool #4* will bring you the greatest depth and benefit from the process.

☐ TOOL #4

INTIMACY RATING:
How Do You Score?

How intimate is your relationship? Rate each of the following 50 items from your *point of view*—privately, on your own.

SCORE: 1 for true
0 for false
½ if the statement is half-true

PERSON A ___Taylor___
(name)

__1__   1.   My partner is truly my best friend.

__1__   2.   My partner sees me as his/her best friend.

__1__   3.   I would rather spend more free time with my partner than with anyone else I know.

__1__   4.   I sense my partner would rather spend more free time with me than with anyone else.

__1__   5.   The more time we spend together, the better our relationship becomes.

_1_ **6.** I can openly express my upset and anger without fear that my partner will react negatively or reject me.

_1_ **7.** My partner freely expresses anger and upset knowing I will not react negatively or reject him/her.

_½_ **8.** My partner and I share the same definition of love and the various actions that demonstrate love.

_1_ **9.** I can initiate sex when I want to, without fear of being criticized or put down.

_1_ **10.** My partner can initiate sex when s/he wants to without fear of rejection from me.

_1_ **11.** When one of us wants sex and the other does not, we still maintain a deep sense of closeness and intimacy without fighting.

_1_ **12.** I understand how my partner prefers to be loved and what makes him/her feel cared for.

_1_ **13.** My partner understands how I prefer to receive love and what makes me feel cared for.

_1_ **14.** When I'm really disturbed or angry, I want to talk with my partner first, before anyone else (family, friends, therapist).

_1_ **15.** When my partner is upset or angry, s/he prefers to talk with me first before anyone else.

_1_ **16.** I could never replace our relationship because of the trust and openness that we have shared.

_1_ **17.** Regardless of what may happen to me, I believe my partner feels that our relationship is irreplaceable.

_1_ **18.** I give my partner positive feedback often and freely.

_1_ **19.** My partner naturally gives me compliments on a frequent basis.

_1_ **20.** I feel safe emotionally with my partner and feel I can honestly be myself.

_1_ **21.** My partner feels emotionally safe with me, and feels s/he can be his/her real self.

next page

119

__ **22.** I still get excited and have a sense of positive anticipation when I know I'll get to see my partner soon.

__ **23.** My partner still gets excited and expresses positive feelings when knowing s/he will get to see me soon.

__ **24.** I am satisfied with our lovemaking and when we have different needs, my partner reaches out to accommodate me.

__ **25.** My partner is satisfied with our lovemaking and when we have different needs, I reach out to accommodate him/her.

__ **26.** In public, we're affectionate, loving, hold hands or put our arms around each other in most places and situations.

__ **27.** In private, we're affectionate, loving, touch one another a lot, give hugs, kisses, and exchange comments of endearment on a regular basis.

__ **28.** We share income and sources of money; we have equal access to our funds and savings.

__ **29.** Decision-making is a joint effort; neither of us dominates or tries to overpower the other (even in areas where we each take separate responsibility).

__ **30.** We operate as a real team (not as two separate individuals or just "roommates").

__ **31.** We share basically the same ideas of what constitutes a healthy marriage, based on common values.

__ **32.** I respect my partner as a person; I value his/her individuality and competence.

__ **33.** My partner respects me as a person and values my individuality and competence.

__ **34.** We share work and household tasks with a sense of good about what we are doing).

__ **35.** In public, I stand up for my partner (even if I have some minor disagreements).

__ **36.** My partner stands up for me in public (even if he/she has some minor disagreements).

37. I consistently act in a way that shows my partner that he/she is the most important person in my life.

38. My partner consistently acts in a way that demonstrates to me that I'm the most important person in his/her life.

39. I feel a secure sense of freedom in our relationship to develop some hobbies, skills, and/or friendships in which my partner is not particularly interested.

40. My partner feels a secure sense of freedom with me so that he/she can develop some hobbies, skills, and/or friendships in which I'm not particularly interested.

41. I feel understood by my partner and trust his/her empathy for my feelings.

42. My partner feels understood by me and trusts my empathy or his/her feelings.

43. When we've had serious problems or crises, we've basically been able to face them together, which has strengthened our relationship.

44. Even when we argue, fight, or have our differences, I still have a sense of good will and trust with my partner.

45. I know my partner still feels my good will and trust even when we argue or fight over our differences.

46. We share a clear vision of our future and look forward to sharing our life together.

47. My partner and I are more "fully alive" when we are together and operating as a team.

48. At times, I've felt like the "giver" of love and understanding, and at other times my partner has felt the same; the important thing is simply BEING THERE for the other person.

49. We both have the capacity to soothe, strengthen, and help to heal the inner hurts and fears of the other.

50. I have the ultimate sense that when "the chips are down," my partner will always come through for me.

PERSONAL NOTES PAGE:
Record your indivdual thoughts, reactions, comments, and questions below.

PERSON B _____ Rob

(name)

Rate each of the following 50 items from your *point of view—*
privately, on your own.

SCORE: 1 for true
   0 for false
   ½ if the statement is half-true

$49\frac{1}{2}$

____ **1.** My partner is truly my best friend.

____ **2.** My partner sees me as his/her best friend.

____ **3.** I would rather spend more free time with my partner than with anyone else I know.

____ **4.** I sense my partner would rather spend more free time with me than with anyone else.

____ **5.** The more time we spend together, the better our relationship becomes.

____ **6.** I can openly express my upset and anger without fear that my partner will react negatively or reject me.

____ **7.** My partner freely expresses anger and upset knowing I will not react negatively or reject him/her.

½ **8.** My partner and I share the same definition of love and the various actions that demonstrate love.

____ **9.** I can initiate sex when I want to, without fear of being criticized or put down.

____ **10.** My partner can initiate sex when s/he wants to without fear of rejection from me.

next page

___ 11. When one of us wants sex and the other does not, we still maintain a deep sense of closeness and intimacy without fighting.

___ 12. I understand how my partner prefers to be loved and what makes him/her feel cared for.

___ 13. My partner understands how I prefer to receive love and what makes me feel cared for.

___ 14. When I'm really disturbed or angry, I want to talk with my partner first, before anyone else (family, friends, therapist).

___ 15. When my partner is upset or angry, s/he prefers to talk with me first before anyone else.

___ 16. I could never replace our relationship because of the trust and openness that we have shared.

___ 17. Regardless of what may happen to me, I believe my partner feels that our relationship is irreplaceable.

___ 18. I give my partner positive feedback often and freely.

___ 19. My partner naturally gives me compliments on a frequent basis.

___ 20. I feel safe emotionally with my partner and feel I can honestly be myself.

___ 21. My partner feels emotionally safe with me, and feels s/he can be his/her real self.

___ 22. I still get excited and have a sense of positive anticipation when I know I'll get to see my partner soon.

___ 23. My partner still gets excited and expresses positive feelings when knowing s/he will get to see me soon.

___ 24. I am satisfied with our lovemaking and when we have different needs, my partner reaches out to accommodate me.

___ 25. My partner is satisfied with our lovemaking and when we have different needs, I reach out to accommodate him/her.

___ 26. In public, we're affectionate, loving, hold hands or put our arms around each other in most places and situations.

27. In private, we're affectionate, loving, touch one another a lot, give hugs, kisses, and exchange comments of endearment on a regular basis.

28. We share income and sources of money; we have equal access to our funds and savings.

29. Decision-making is a joint effort; neither of us dominates or tries to overpower the other (even in areas where we each take separate responsibility).

30. We operate as a real team (not as two separate individuals or just "roommates").

31. We share basically the same ideas of what constitutes a healthy marriage, based on common values.

32. I respect my partner as a person; I value his/her individuality and competence.

33. My partner respects me as a person and values my individuality and competence.

34. We share work and household tasks with a sense of good about what we are doing).

35. In public, I stand up for my partner (even if I have some minor disagreements).

36. My partner stands up for me in public (even if he/she has some minor disagreements).

37. I consistently act in a way that shows my partner that he/she is the most important person in my life.

38. My partner consistently acts in a way that demonstrates to me that I'm the most important person in his/her life.

39. I feel a secure sense of freedom in our relationship to develop some hobbies, skills, and/or friendships in which my partner is not particularly interested.

40. My partner feels a secure sense of freedom with me so that he/she can develop some hobbies, skills, and/or friendships in which I'm not particularly interested.

next page

41. I feel understood by my partner and trust his/her empathy for my feelings.

42. My partner feels understood by me and trusts my empathy or his/her feelings.

43. When we've had serious problems or crises, we've basically been able to face them together, which has strengthened our relationship.

44. Even when we argue, fight, or have our differences, I still have a sense of good will and trust with my partner.

45. I know my partner still feels my good will and trust even when we argue or fight over our differences.

46. We share a clear vision of our future and look forward to sharing our life together.

47. My partner and I are more "fully alive" when we are together and operating as a team.

48. At times, I've felt like the "giver" of love and understanding, and at other times my partner has felt the same; the important thing is simply BEING THERE for the other person.

49. We both have the capacity to soothe, strengthen, and help to heal the inner hurts and fears of the other.

50. I have the ultimate sense that when "the chips are down," my partner will always come through for me.

PERSONAL NOTES PAGE:

Record your indivdual thoughts, reactions, comments, and questions below.

SCORING

After rating each item (1 is true, 0 is false, ½ for half-true), add your total points. Each item is 2 % of your rating; for example, if you have 32 items marked true, and 2 items marked ½ , your percentage rating is 33 x 2 = 66%

TOTAL NUMBER FOR **PERSON A:**
OF TRUE ITEMS __49½__ x 2 = __99__ % (Total Score)

TOTAL NUMBER FOR **PERSON B:** 99
OF TRUE ITEMS __49½__ x 2 = __99__ % (Total Score)

SUMMARY OF PERCENTAGE RATINGS

♥ **90% to 100%** = Very intimate, an outstanding relationship in which intimacy is high and most any problem can be resolved, often without counseling or with short-term intervention.

―― **75% to 89%** = A few major problems that need attention and correction. With diligence and concerted effort from both partners, the relationship can definitely become more intimate and rewarding. Basically a "good relationship" but needs some work.

―― **60% to 74%** = Some significant problems, lack of depth-intimacy, with major communication breakdown; serious concerns requiring some major and perhaps painful changes and the willingness to learn new ways of dealing with one another; strong and consistent intervention (e.g., confrontative couples' therapy).

―― **40% to 59%** = Borderline relationship requiring major "emotional surgery," perhaps even some unusual "emergency" stop-gap measures or "crisis intervention" may be needed before intense couples' therapy can begin. Some powerful changes are needed; however, the relationship still has some solid potential.

―― **0% to 39%** = Must question WHY you are together! Is the relationship going to be permanently more painful and frustrating than it is safe and pleasurable? Under what conditions or agreements should the two people remain together? Is it possible to actually repair this relationship? Are both partners actually willing to do major, confrontative therapy and to change certain aspects of themselves?

DISCUSSION FOR COUPLES

1) After each partner has taken the survey alone and computed her/his *percentage rating*, share your scores with one another. *Go over each item together* and explain to your partner WHY you put true or false (include examples; things you feel are *missing* from your intimacy, things you and/or your partner might work on, improve, or change, as well as *appreciations* and *special things* your partner has done to make you feel good and/or understood).

2) Discussion of the items should not extend over ONE HOUR PER WEEK. For many couples, the hour might better be broken into 15- or 30-minute segments. Even if you only cover several of the items, STOP after 15 or 30 minutes and ASSESS THE TIME. Make a "date" for your next discussion. (Most couples can fully discuss 6 to 9 items in one hour.)

3) Do not get defensive or upset, cry, throw "temper tantrums," or display negative reactions/criticism to your partner's explanation; this is only a vehicle to help you UNDERSTAND each other better, not to create more distance. Instead, take turns doing "MIRRORING" (i.e., active listening) and accurately reflect back to your partner what he/she is saying from HIS/HER point of view. *No argument, no debate*—only listening and understanding should be your mutual goal in order to create more intimacy.

5

BATTLE BETWEEN THE SEXES:
Guidelines for "Getting It"

When I was developing this *Tool*, a great deal of research had recently been published regarding biological and genetic differences in temperament between the sexes. These factors were expressed in personality and emotional responses in males and females. I needed to convey the essence of this research to my therapy couples.

To do this effectively, I eventually created a three-part Fact Sheet that became part of this *Tool #5*

1) **Research Summary: Male and Female Differences**

2) **What Happens in Relationships**

3) **Suggestions for Better Communication**

This Fact Sheet became the basis for the two partners to learn more about themselves and each other. It also encouraged greater objectivity and a more realistic look at what was happening during their fights and arguments.

Finally, as we put this new knowledge to use, it would become necessary to change certain behaviors and/or patterns. At times this was painful for the couples who needed some "emotional surgery" on their relationship; the consciousness about *male-female differences* was basically missing among these clients.

MEN IN "FIGHT OR FLIGHT"

One couple commented with amazement that they "couldn't believe the difference it made" when they established the habit "of *not* discussing a problem or conflict for at least fifteen minutes after it first arose."

This particular couple, Carolyn and Brent, achieved rapid growth after putting this "habit change" into practice. Carolyn said she "never realized that Brent actually felt trapped and criticized" in the face of her demands to "talk about this immediately." She became strongly empathetic to the "male's reaction" and was willing to back off and discipline herself to wait out the fifteen minutes (or whatever the period was) until the agreed upon "appointment time" (always within the next 24 hours).

Brent became much more relaxed around Carolyn and said he "didn't suffer so much from flight-or-flight adrenalin rushes." He felt "safer" and more able to discuss problems, in response to her willingness to give him the "space" he needed.

They later learned more refined skills, as they practiced "active listening" and developed the habit of accurately "mirroring" back the partner's intended message (including her/his attitude and meaning).

BATTLING NEIGHBORS

Another couple—I'll call them Bill and Cheryl—were not therapy clients of mine but acquaintances who were next-door neighbors. It was summer, and we were all doing a lot of barbecuing outside. It was impossible not to hear their vociferous arguments with each other.

At one point Bill actually walked around the fence to apologize. He said, "The whole neighborhood could probably hear us arguing."

He seemed agitated and embarrassed, and I invited him to have a seat on our porch. In an attempt to offer him some comfort, I said, "That's okay. My husband and I still fight, and I'm a marriage counselor, to boot."

His jaw dropped so far, I might have been admitting I was from another planet. "You mean you still have fights with Eddie? But he's such a great guy."

After agreeing with his assessment of my husband, I added, "It's not so great when I trigger his feelings of being trapped . . . or blamed for whatever. . . ."

Bill looked stunned. How could I be doing marriage counseling when I still had fights with my own husband? I explained that I'd been a therapist for almost 29 years. And that I was working on a "new *Tool*" to help couples get through impasses just like the one he and Cheryl had—or Eddie and I—or any of the other couples in the neighborhood.

Bill wanted to know what this "*Tool*" was. "Maybe a big hammer to hit each other over the head?"

We both had a good laugh at this idea. Then I explained that men and women are constructed differently emotionally and have different sets of needs. All too often, this sets them on a "collision course" when both of them are under stress, feeling blamed or trapped in an emotional conflict. I told Bill I was working on ways to help both partners avoid these all-too-common fights and the accompanying habitual and repetitive arguments.

I asked Bill if he'd like to see my rough copy of this *Tool*.

Seeing his perplexed and slightly skeptical look, I ran inside and grabbed two copies. I offered Bill one and wrote Cheryl's name on the other.

"What do you say, Bill, would you help me out with this, be my test case?"

I explained that I was trying to find out if this *Tool* (i.e., my Fact Sheet) could be of any benefit to him and Cheryl as a couple. If they were willing to give it a try, I said, it would be best for each of them to read the sheet alone and then re-read it together. I suggested each of them use a different colored marker to highlight the facts that struck them as personally most relevant.

Bill agreed to "give it a whirl" and said he knew Cheryl "would love this relationship stuff." He made his way back around the fence carrying the two pages.

Almost two weeks went by, during which neither Eddie nor I ran into either of then. Then one evening Cheryl saw me picking up our mail and hurried over to say, "Those pages you gave us were a miracle!"

After carefully reading through my Fact Sheet, both of them felt much greater empathy for the other and realized how their habitual actions had caused the other to "feel defensive, neglected [Cheryl] or trapped [Bill]."

They made a clear decision to stop some of the most offensive patterns that seemed to stress-out their partner. For example, Cheryl declared she would *stop all demands* for Bill *to have "immediate talks"* when she was upset. Instead, she requested an "appointment" with Bill (usually for 10 minutes) within the next 24 hours. This way, he would not feel "verbally stampeded, blamed for something, or trapped" by her emotionally.

For his part, Bill agreed to "keep the appointment" (usually the following morning, for 10 minutes). He also volunteered to *self-correct* his angry and defensive tone when he felt accused or "verbally attacked" by Cheryl. He would no longer walk away in silence, knowing he was causing her to feel neglected and unloved. Instead, Bill agreed to give her a big silent hug and remind her of their coming "appointment time."

It worked. They became much happier as a couple. I cannot remember ever again overhearing a fight from across the fence.

RESOURCES FOR FURTHER STUDY

Some great books to help couples became available during this era. Among them were John Grey's *Men Are from Mars, Women Are from Venus*, a clear explanation of the basic and more structural differences between the sexes.

Another gem is *How to Improve Your Marriage without Talking about It,* by Patricia Love, Ed.D. and Steven Stosny, Ph.D. It made clear the point that many women, with their continual "verbal harangues," push their male partners into either a passive-aggressive silence or an angry, defensive posture guaranteed to produce more distance.

The persistent *use* and *implementation* of these *Tools* can lead to much deeper caring and greater satisfaction in male-female relationships. It's the actual *practice* of them, on a daily basis, that makes for enduring qualitative change.

Let's see if the Fact Sheet from *Tool #5* can help you understand your partner at a deeper level. Try studying the "Facts" together, as a couple.

⊡ TOOL #5

BATTLE BETWEEN THE SEXES:
Guidelines for "Getting It"

RESEARCH SUMMARY:

Following is a brief summary of facts regarding Male and Female Differences

1) Females

2) Males

3) What Happens in Relationships

DIRECTIONS I:

1) First use a *colored marker* to *underline* (or circle or check) all sentences that really strike your interest, or that might be relevent in your current life situation.

2) On the *same pages* ask your partner to use a marker of *another color* to underline (or circle) all the sentences he/she feels are relevant.

1) FEMALES:

A) When baby girls are anxious or stressed, they make eye contact to establish connection and find comfort.

B) Girls are more easily startled than boys (e.g., by a loud noise or sudden impact).

C) Girls and women want to *talk* about issues, thus forming a bond to alleviate stress.

D) Women feel increasing stress when male partners refuse to look at them (have eye contact) and discuss her emotions.

E) Women want to verbally bond with their mates; they believe discussing stressful topics will increase intimacy.

2) MALES:

A) When baby boys feel stressed or anxious, they look around with a fight-or-flight response.

B) Baby boys have intense "startle" reactions, which increase adrenalin; they need to *act* on this (fight) or withdraw (flight) to alleviate the agitation and anxiety.

C) Boys or men are driven under stress to act on adrenalin rushes; if they cannot, they withdraw to cool down and regain equilibrium.

D) Men naturally want to *do* for their mate, not talk about it.

E) Men feel more stress when the partner insists on discussing her stressful concerns.

3) WHAT HAPPENS IN RELATIONSHIPS:

A) Women need to talk about their stress, especially relationship problems, thus forming a bond.

B) A man believes his mate's stress (complaints) indicate something is wrong with him and/or that he is inadequate to do anything about it. He feels he does not measure up to her standards, is doing things incorrectly, etc.

C) In extremely uncomfortable situations, a man's adrenaline and fight-or-flight response kicks in. He may become aggressive (fight) or withdraw completely (flight) to soothe his agitation.

D) In the same situation a woman feels increasing stress when her mate ignores her, walks out, shouts at her or otherwise threatens their bond of intimacy and safety.

E) Men feel trapped and angry when they feel blamed and powerless to do anything about it. They see no benefit in talking about it more.

DIRECTIONS II:
Discuss HOW and WHY some of the above facts (that you have circled or underlined) actually apply to your relationship and/or your life situation—and perhaps the reasons you each respond the way you do. Then proceed to DIRECTIONS III.

* * *

DIRECTIONS III:
Following your discussion of the 3 sets of FACTS, then *decide together* which of the 7 suggestions on the following page— if any—could be helpful for making your relationship more satisfying.

SUGGESTIONS FOR BETTER COMMUNICATION

1) In times of relationship stress or anxiety, talking about "the problem" immediately *may make things worse.*

2) The closest form of intimacy occurs when *not* talking. When deeply connected, *men* talk more and *women* talk less.

3) Holding the partner in silence with a sense of caring sometimes works wonders for both sexes.

4) It is helpful when the couple can agree on a sign (e.g., a special word or hand signal) to keep the stress from escalating.

5) When either partner (usually the woman) feels they *must discuss* an issue, they can ask for an "appointment." Both must agree to a specific time for the duration of the appointment (between 5 and 30 minutes) to occur within the following 24 hours.

6) It is best to use a *neutral tone* of voice and *neutral language,* avoiding phrases like "you never," "you always," etc.

7) Practice *active listening* without interruption or projection of your own feelings:
   - Take turns communicating only *one* idea at a time.
   - *Repeat* the other's intended message, beginning with "I heard you say . . ." until your partner is satisfied that he/she has been heard accurately.

6

GETTING TO KNOW YOU:
Sentence Completion

The pressing need to gather a lot of information quickly within the traditional 50-minute therapy session was the primary force that led to my invention of *Tool #6*. It was necessary to gain a "big-picture overview" without becoming mired in the details or emotionality of each response.

I began structuring certain sentences around specific problems for individual couples. Then I expanded the process to include specific sentences only as "homework," designed for that couple's unique circumstances. Clients were instructed to have only "one or two 15-minute period(s)" of sentence completion between therapy sessions.

The "rules" for this exercise are *stricter* than those for any of the other *Tools*. Each partner takes his/her turn by simply completing the sentence. No discussion or explanation or elaboration is allowed. Each assigned sentence is completed three (or up to five) times, with the partners taking turns.

At times, it was extremely difficult for a participant not to explode or explain a certain statement; it could be equally hard for the listener to express nothing or simply say, "Thank you."

FULL DISCLOSURE, NO "WITHHOLDS"

In relation to this exercise, I'm reminded of a warm and attentive lesbian couple I had been counseling over several months. Emily and Connie were well suited in many ways and enjoyed the benefit of mutual trust, loyalty, a no-exit philosophy and support from extended family on both sides.

Emily had insisted on having artificial insemination to become pregnant almost two years prior to the couple's first session with me. As a result, they became the proud parents of a healthy baby boy, Nick, now almost one year old.

Being the birth mother was exciting and fulfilling for Emily. Connie was also "on board," loved parenting and seemed happy with her title of "Mommy-two." At the same time Connie became extremely worried about finances, Nick's future education, his retirement income and similar issues—her chronic concerns.

Emily had commented earlier, "Connie has always been a little paranoid over future finances." She assured Connie that her own teaching position would always assure them "some steady income and great health insurance as a family."

Connie, a middle-management executive in a textile company, had a higher salary than Emily but with "slowly dwindling benefits." Emily kept reassuring Connie that Nick's retirement income was *not* an issue; after all, he was barely one year old!

I was able to assuage Connie's serious concern over Nick's future retirement by showing her how establishing an account with a large insurance company and depositing approximately $2,000 annually on each of Nick's birthdays, beginning at age 1 (compounding all dividends and interest, with no withdrawals for any reason) would set up for him, by the time he was in his 60s, well over a million dollars. (I referred her to a good agent.) Both

Connie and Emily were satisfied with this investment plan; this area of their problems was easily resolved.

The more complex issue was Connie's increasing agitation. During Emily's pregnancy and childbirth, Connie became so worried and upset about finances that a couple of her executive colleagues, who sincerely supported and respected her "gay family," offered her a way to relax—just to take "a few snorts of cocaine."

Connie's colleagues claimed they used the drug "regularly, in very small amounts, just to feel better." They felt sure it would "take the pressure off her," maybe help her relax and "not be so paranoid." Eventually, Connie agreed to try the cocaine, hoping it would help her feel better.

But now she worried even more about the cocaine. It was a drug, an *illegal drug*. She had used it only about "three times . . . with her two strongly supportive colleagues" before deciding it was not for her. When she explained her feelings to them, they supported her completely and promised never to mention it again. This felt great, and she was relieved to be "done with the experiment."

But Connie was now stuck with the "secret"—the *only* secret she had ever kept from Emily. She now felt "really paranoid" over her responsibility to share the truth about this with Emily.

I had one private session with Connie in which she confessed to feeling a lot of stress and worry over "becoming a family." She and Emily had both wanted a child for the entire fourteen years of their committed relationship. Emily had been especially preoccupied with this idea. After studying all possibilities for gay couples to adopt, Emily finally settled on herself having a child through artificial insemination. With this option, they would be able to choose the physical characteristics, I.Q. and genetic history of the "donor." They were ecstatically happy over their decision.

At the same time, Connie began her usual worry over the financial future of the child, his or her college education, health benefits, etc. Emily had often expressed dismay over Connie's "paranoia" and claimed it "drained some of the joy" from their adoration and commitment to the baby.

RESOLUTION

I saw an opportunity to resolve this nebulous discomfort and distance between Emily and Connie by directing Sentence Completions (*Tool #6*) between them. In one particular (joint) counseling session, an eruption occurred because of two particular sentences: 1) "I prefer it when you . . ." and 2) "I feel uncomfortable when you . . . " What they experienced was an avalanche of emotional breakthrough.

Emily had expressed concern over her vague feeling that Connie was "holding out on her." Connie responded hesitantly, "Yes. For the first and only time in our fourteen-year relationship, I've kept a secret from you." Emily was aghast and curious. What could this possibly be?

Connie slowly and quietly explained the entire cocaine story in detail, delineating how her two supportive colleagues had tried to help with her "up-tight worry." Both of them, Connie explained, occasionally used "recreational cocaine" just to party and relax. But she herself soon discovered that she "wasn't cut out for this remedy" and asked her friends never to bring up the subject again. All this had taken place about six months earlier.

Emily expressed relief that Connie's cocaine experience was safely in the past and even greater relief that Connie had finally decided to share her secret.

"We've never had any secrets from one another," Emily said.

"Through all our ups and downs over the years, this has been our first 'withhold.' I'm so glad it's all over now."

Emily's relief at the disclosure seemed to trigger an outpouring to her partner: "I know you had all this stress and worry only because you love me and our baby so very much. . . . Connie, Honey, I just want you to relax and enjoy us more, rather than worrying. I know your two colleagues socially and have been impressed with their unconditional support of our marriage and family. I can see how they were only trying to help with your concerns.

"I can easily forgive them—and forgive you—for experimenting with the cocaine. Hell, it's difficult for anyone becoming a parent for the first time. Let's just do a 'start-over.' Okay?"

Connie was massively relieved. She cried, and they hugged each other tightly for several minutes. As far as I know, things went very well for the new family following our sessions.

NEVER LISTENING, ALWAYS INTERRUPTING

Here is a typical example of the potency of *Tool #6*. Guy and Erma (married for 40 years, ages 66 and 67) came to me for "communication counseling."

Erma claimed she had been "feeling depressed for a number of years . . . because Guy never listens." He was in the habit of interrupting Erma continually, "taking over" her every time she tried to express something he disagreed with.

Guy had been a high-powered, aggressive salesman who was determined to control every conversation. Erma was "very tired" of trying to cope with his apparent need to control almost everything she said.

Guy's low level of self-awareness and his obliviousness as to how he affected his wife was clear. I asked if he had ever been exposed to "active listening" in his extensive sales career.

"No," he said, "and I'm not that interested now."

I asked if he was interested in saving his marriage.

He got a quizzical look on his face and slowly answered, "Yes . . . I guess that's why Erma had me come in here."

"That's right," I said. "In a marriage, *both* partners need to be heard and understood." I went on to explain the concept of "active listening," the importance of not "talking over" the other person, and how crucial it was to have a sincere desire to understand and nurture the partner.

Guy acted as if this was news to him, even though he had been "married forty long years." At first he was defensive, telling me he knew Erma "better than any other person on earth."

I agreed with his statement, adding that it was now time to "get underneath . . . to actually *feel* what Erma must be feeling . . . to experience her frustration and anger over never being *listened to* . . . to comprehend how 'shut off' and 'put down' she must feel."

Guy had never thought of *his wife* having opinions or feelings separate from his own. As we explored this further, it became clear that he sincerely felt Erma was a mere reflection of him and should always be aligned with his beliefs and opinions. Of course, she had "her little areas, inside the home and with the kids" where she "had some decision-making to do . . . because I was too busy to be bothered."

It was slowly getting through to Guy that Erma was in need of "more respect" and "more personal freedom" from him. He was stunned.

I gave them both copies of *Tool #6, GETTING TO KNOW YOU: Sentence Completion,* and asked that they read the directions.

This would require some discipline and restraint from both parties: *taking turns without any response* from the partner (or only a simple "Thank you").

Erma's eyes lit up as she finally felt safe to speak her own truth. Guy was hesitant, then acted as if he were about to blow a fuse when Erma finally said, "The truth about our relationship is . . . that you try to control everything I say."

Guy was silent for a long moment, then took his turn, stating that "The truth about our relationship is that . . . I love you very much."

As the process went on, Guy's eyes kept filling with tears. Apologies were meager at first, but suddenly he burst into an emotional explanation of his "need to control Erma" (completely disregarding Directions for the **Tool**).

I went with his reaction, encouraging him to "go deeper" and explain more about his deep-seated need to control. It turned out that Erma was just one area in which he felt the need for total control. He explained that in "the vast area of sales, it's not possible to control the variables . . . . But with my own wife, she's just a part of me, and a reflection of *who* I am. . . ."

Guy's inability to see Erma as a person separate from himself became evident as we talked further. I assured him, as did Erma, that she was, indeed, a separate person. Although they had been married 40 years, she still had the right to her own feelings and opinions, which sometimes were different from his.

This fact really was "news" to Guy. He had never thought about it. A whole new area of "rights" and "freedom" opened up in his mind regarding Erma. He did sincerely love her and had no idea how much he had stifled and manipulated her.

We would go back to **Tool #6** as Guy's communication skills slowly improved. Over the next several months of counseling and the use of many **Tools** (some of which I wrote specifically for Guy and Erma), their love truly did thrive and grow more intense. Guy became a more sensitive listener.

They invited me to attend a service that included the renewal of their wedding vows on their 41st anniversary.

RULES FOR TOOL #6

There were many different couples for whom this *Tool* proved to be especially potent and essential for the improvement of their relationship.

It's important to mention that the "rules" or directions for completing these sentences in *Tool #6* can be *extremely restrictive*. This exercise is more structured and disciplined than any of the others, and that holds true whether the couple uses the sentences in a therapy session or at home. The rules include: *no interrupting, no reacting, no explaining, no defending.*

Each partner simply takes his/her turn completing the designated sentence. Period. The only acceptable form of response is a simple "Thank you." This setup creates a situation in which each partner can actually listen objectively to the other's statements. The process allows the therapist and the couple to gather a lot of information about both partners in a short time.

Sometimes we do not know where the use of any specific *Tool* will take us. And at times, the feelings that can arise might catch the participants off guard. My hope is that, in the end, it all works toward greater awareness and empathy—making your love thrive.

Try out *Tool #6* and see where it takes you and your partner.

▣ TOOL #6

GETTING TO KNOW YOU:
Sentence Completion

Plan to do this process, as a couple, for no longer than 15 minutes at a time. And no more total time than *one hour* per week (a maximum possibility of 4 sessions).

Set aside a 15-minute period in which the two of you will take turns completing the following sentences; to begin, you will each complete sentence #1, then each complete it again, from 3 to 5 times—taking turns.

This continues for no more than 5 times before moving on to the next sentence. Some couples will complete 3 or 4 of the sentences, others might do 8 or 9 within the 15-minute period. Experiment with a comfortable pace for you as a couple.

The rules for this exercise are strict:

1) When one person is speaking, the partner shows no reaction and moves on to speak only during his/her own turn.

2) The only appropriate response is to say *"Thank you."* *No other reaction is allowed* (e.g., no interrupting, no explaining, no comments).

3) Do not allow this exercise to continue *beyond* the 15 minutes per session—and a *total* of 1-hour per week.

In subsequent sessions, you can pick up where you left off (e.g., if you ended with sentence #5 in your first session, you could pick up with #6 in your second session)—with both of you completing each sentence 3 to 5 times, taking turns.

#1. "The truth about our relationship is . . ."

#2. "One thing I appreciate about you is . . ."

#3. "One thing I sometimes resent about you is . . ."

#4. "One thing I especially like about our relationship is . . ."

#5. "I prefer it when you . . ."

#6. "I feel uncomfortable when you . . ."

#7. "It would help me if you would . . ."

#8. "I feel loved when you . . ."

#9. "I feel rejected when you . . ."

#10. "The real truth about our relationship is . . ."

NOTES PAGE:

Record your indivdual thoughts, reactions, comments, and questions below.

7

SUBTYPES:
The Hidden Level of Personality

The "Subtype" is a deeper level of mostly unconscious personality. It is buried in the automatic knee-jerk reactions that we all have on a daily basis. Because Subtype is not conscious in the same way many other personality traits are, it can confuse us and catch us off guard.

Due to the unconscious nature of Subtypes, they must be analyzed and studied *per se*. They must be looked at objectively, with the differences between them clearly understood.

In my four decades of marriage counseling, I've found that couples who have *different* Subtypes (rather than belonging to the same Subtype) have a higher probability of misunderstanding and communication breakdowns. However, when couples share the mindset and unconscious motives of the *same* Subtype, their empathy for and acceptance of the partner comes more naturally and automatically.

Along my journey of studying personality theory and the Enneagram, I quickly learned about Subtypes. I was struck by how different a person's intended message could be from what the partner actually heard. The confusion of "intent" with the understood "meaning" of a message can lead to major misunderstandings.

Tool #7 is designed to explain and shed light on some of these issues.

THE THREE SUBTYPES

1) Self-Preservation

2) Sexual-Fusion

3) Social.

The most detailed and helpful explanations can be found in Don Riso and Russ Hudson's definitive book, *The Wisdom of the Enneagram*. (In their book, they refer to Subtypes as "Instinctual Variants," which is a more precise term.)

Numerous other Enneagram authors have explored the use of Subtypes to further explain largely unconscious personality differences.

Tool #7, Subtypes, addresses only a part of the personality that gets buried beneath the many layers of more conscious traits, motives and fears. *Subtype* is thought to be a set of unconsciously learned defenses and strategies, essentially acquired in early childhood. They are acquired from the many events, traumas and dramas in our first six-to-ten years of life.

The study and understanding of our own and our partner's *Subtype* can provide us with help and insight into many of our hurt feelings, anger and communication breakdowns.

It appears that the three *Subtypes* are equally and randomly distributed in the population and among all personality types. It is reasonable to assume that approximately two-thirds of all couples *do not* share the same *Subtype*.

The one-third of all couples who *do* share the same *Subtype* often benefit from the *mutual biases* they have in the unconscious creation of their motives and viewpoints.

WHY AREN'T YOU MORE LIKE ME?

The majority of couples who have *different Subtypes* have more difficulty in understanding why their partner can have "such knee-jerk-responses." This doesn't make sense! As one client put it, "I couldn't make any sense out of Sue; then I studied her *Subtype*."

Having different Subtypes can create major communication problems. Two different sets of strategies-defenses-intentions are sometimes in conflict. This can play havoc in any committed relationship.

The painful early years of my own marriage offer a case in point. My husband, Eddie, is a *Self-Preservation Subtype*, while I am in the *Sexual-Fusion* group. I would often feel neglected, as if he didn't care about my concerns or intentions. However, there was little doubt about how he would meet his own needs. For example, in most social situations he would plan how he could get comfortable, then have an "exit strategy," usually geared toward leaving as early as possible.

At the same time, I was happy to be with him and longed for his undivided attention (which usually got transferred back to his personal needs). I can recall many times when I wanted to "be a couple" and focus primarily on our relationship.

The available food, room temperature and other environmental details didn't matter much to me, so long as I could be with him. My need to sustain this one-to-one connection frequently resulted in disappointment.

My dismay was amplified by his occasional requests for me to stop "fussing" over him or not "focus" on him—leave him *alone* (so as not to interrupt his concentration).

He responded with utter disbelief when I complained about feeling neglected or rejected or just not being part of his "awareness."

This would usually produce shock and chagrin on his part.

He often responded defensively with, "You know I love you, Mona. I'm always with you," or with exasperated questions such as, "Can't you see I'm thinking?" and "Don't you need to focus more on yourself?"

This is typical of the dialogue between partners when one is a *Self-Preservation Subtype* and the other is a *Sexual-Fusion Subtype*. It seems obvious that having different *Subtype* perspectives can make communication more difficult and frustrating. Sharing the same *Subtype* can make the intended message more understandable and acceptable.

I must point out that, while this is generally true, there are always exceptions. One was apparent in a young engaged couple who *shared* the Sexual-Fusion Subtype. They both had a severe problem with jealousy that resulted in continual accusations (e.g., flirting with others, potential affairs, "secret" rendezvous). Their mutual need to connect was obvious, but their bouts of jealous rage ended in a painful breakup.

In general, couples who have different *Subtypes* need to understand why their conflicts occur and work to deepen their empathy for one another.

THE DISAPPEARING WIFE

A typical example was Heather and Alex, married eight years with two children ages 1 and 5. Alex was a high-powered salesman of medical equipment with wide smiles and handshakes for everyone, a *Social Subtype*. Heather was more introverted, grounded within herself, and protective of her immediate surroundings. Her being a *Self-Preservation Subtype* often caused conflict, especially when she and Alex were in "any group situation."

In our counseling session Heather lamented that Alex "is always on! In any group of people, he feels compelled to 'work the room'; he feels he must get around to everyone there." This predictable behavior of her husband's exhausted Heather.

She was more concerned about "getting home on time for the kids." Having enough sleep and being able to summon the necessary energy for chores and appointments were constant worries for her.

Several years before she came to see me, Heather had become so disengaged at a large social gala where Alex was "sure he could make some good connections" that she left in the middle of the party and drove herself home.

Alex was so busy meeting everyone, "selling when he could" and enjoying small talk with new acquaintances (mostly orthopedists) that he didn't even realize Heather was missing.

As the party was ending, he looked around, noticed her absence and realized their car was also missing. After a moment of slight panic, he called her on her cell phone.

"Yes, dear Alex, I've been home for over two hours. Could you find a ride home with someone?"

He did and was able to make another sales pitch to the doctor who drove him home.

Heather had proved her point: Whenever Alex got into a group—any group—she became invisible. Her needs and desires didn't matter to "Mr. Social Alex."

Alex appeared stunned as I explained the dynamics of their different Subtypes and how our biases, strategies and "blind spots" can produce significant pain and hurt for a spouse.

Both Heather and Alex were excellent "therapy students." Each of them eventually demonstrated a high degree of empathy and compassion for the other, and both were grateful to understand the *actual motives* of their partner. Alex especially appreciated Heather's "good sense" regarding their home, health issues, diet, care of the children, etc. Heather was thankful for Alex's drive to "earn a lot of money" to keep them at such a high standard of living so she didn't have to work.

They were happy—and agreed to "review these *Subtypes*" on a monthly basis.

A COUPLE IN CRISIS

A far more complicated example was the case of Zara and Nadar, who had immigrated to the United States from Iran with their respective parents some 25 years earlier. Their common culture and family background bound them together, and they had a solid marriage in many ways. Zara had just turned 42 and owned a small dress shop, which she loved. Nadar, 38, also had an independent business selling imported Persian rugs.

They requested marriage counseling in order to solve their only issue: Zara's cancer. She had been recently diagnosed with aggressive breast cancer, which threw her into a tailspin about what to do.

Why had they chosen to counsel with *me*?

All the traditional medical options were racing through her mind: surgery, chemo, radiation, etc. Plus, she had been talking with two of her customers (who had become her closest friends) about the many "alternative" treatments: the well-known clinics in Mexico, I.V. detox treatments, macrobiotic diets, supplements, etc. The plethora of options was overwhelming.

As a *Sexual-Fusion Subtype*, Zara felt deeply connected to her two best friends, each of whom tried to help by pushing her in a different direction.

Nadar was shocked, almost paralyzed with distress over Zara's cancer. He needed her as his stabilizer, to keep him "on track," well fed, well dressed and financially secure. He was a *Self-Preservation Subtype* and depended on her to help keep his world grounded and predictable. What would he ever do if, "God forbid," she succumbed to the disease?

My first concern was to find an excellent medical counselor specializing in "cancer options" to help them navigate their way through the many confusing choices. I also explained that I could counsel them only on *relationship* issues.

They quickly explained that Nadar had no time for Zara's two best friends, who had been former dress shop customers. He wanted Zara to consult only him and her doctors. He could see no value in her continued "blabbing" with her girlfriends.

Zara felt heartbroken. Couldn't he understand how important her friends were, especially at a time like this? The friends had worked hard to gather information, books and websites on the various cancer treatments available. After all, they were on her side, just as Nadar was.

Nadar incessantly explained that he and she "had no time and no energy to waste." It was imperative that they "pull in their resources"—especially their *time* and *energy*—and buckle down to "curing this damn cancer."

As they self-acknowledged their Subtypes, I had an opportunity to explain to Nadar how important Zara's "two best friends" were to her. It would be to *his* advantage, I pointed out, to team up with her friends, since they were informed about many cancer treatments he was unfamiliar with.

He accepted the wisdom of this and benefitted also from listening as I explained his Self-Preservation nature to Zara. He was proud of his protective stance and decided that including her two best friends in their "circle of protection" would be helpful to her.

She was relieved to have Nadar embrace her friends and all the good information they had gathered. As his attitude became more inclusive, she made him promise to "make all four of us the executive decision-making committee, with *me* as president."

About a year later I learned that Zara had opted for a surgical mastectomy, with no further traditional medical treatment. Instead, she completed an alternative cancer program (mostly strict diet, extensive I.V. infusions and supplements) in Mexico. One of her friends told me she was doing fine and was planning to re-open her beloved dress shop.

Her friend also reported that Zara was much happier with Nadar, now that she had come to understand his "Self-Preservation" nature. In return, Nadar came to a deeper acceptance and awareness of how "Sexual-Fusion" functioned in Zara's personality.

I hope you and your partner will study your Subtypes and gain valuable insights from *Tool #7.*

▣ TOOL #7

SUBTYPES:
The Hidden Level of Personality

Begin by studying the following 3-part chart of the *SUBTYPES*.

Ask yourself which of these 3 columns most describes your "knee jerk" reactions—how you automatically *focus your attention* without even thinking about it.

Having the same *SUBTYPE*— the same unconscious focus of attention—leads to much agreement and a common perspective. On the other hand, couples with *different SUBTYPES* have more unconscious differences in priorities, perspective, and values. This often leads to certain kinds of communication breakdowns.

It appears that *SUBTYPE* is randomly distributed in the general population and across all personality Types. As a result, statistacally—two thirds of us have marriage partners/mates that have significant differences in perspective and world view. Explore these differences as objectively as you can.

SELF-PRESERVATION	SEXUAL-FUSION	SOCIAL
(1/3 pop.) Focus on "Survival" What about me? How am I doing?	(1/3 pop.) Focus on "Intimacy." What about the relationship? Soulmate?	(1/3 pop.) Focus on "Community" What about the group/system?
— SELF —	**— US —**	**— GROUP —**
Desires security & safety. Fears not surviving. Seeks survival mechanisms Food, Temperature, Clothes, Comfort, Insurance, Health, Scarce resources.	Desires intensity and connection. Fears being undesirable. Seeks oneness with the other: Mating, Dating, Best Friends, Partners (e.g., like sockets and plugs looking to connect).	Desires social acceptance and recognition. Fears not belonging. Seeks the Clan, Tribe, Social Groups or Party. Inherent awareness of Others as a unit.
• Energy is stable, solid.	• Energy is intense, searching.	• Energy is split, scattered.
• Body is grounded, self-contained.	• Direct eye contact, locks in with intensity.	• Inclusive, adaptive, cooperative, superficial.
• Expects to have environment adjusted to meet their needs.	• Merging, highly charged.	• Aware of power structure, struggles and appropriateness.
• How can I regulate conditions around me and my resources to ensuring comfort and survival?"	• Passion, plugs into intimacy and needs more "juice."	• Focus on welfare of others; adapts self to environment to get acceptance.
• "I must feel secure before giving to others."	• "How do we as a couple (union, relationship) function?"	• "We're all in this together." "Let's leave a legacy."
• "I must "pull in" my energy to protect myself.	• "Who's worth talking to?"	• Let's treat everyone as a group-unit.
	• "Where are the real connections?"	

DIRECTIONS FOR TOOL #7:

1. Study the three different Subtypes, described on the previous page.

2. Decide which one is dominant for you and which is for your partner.

   Note: Everyone has elements of all three in their personality. However, one dominates, a second supports it, and the third is least developed.

3. Discuss how the differences (or sameness) between you influence your communication, both positively and negatively.

4. Since the Subtype is basically unconscious, it can produce many "knee-jerk" reactions. Decide what types of responses you would like to bring to your consciousness, and perhaps gain greater control over your reactions.

8

COMPATIBILITY RATING:
How Compatible Are You?

Kent, 32 and Eleanor, 30, a stunningly beautiful couple, had been engaged for two years and felt deep warmth and affection for one another.

"We've come to you for help," Kent said, acknowledging the apprehension he felt over a marriage commitment. The two of them, he told me, had "no common interests, no common hobbies, no common goals."

"Kent's right," Eleanor said. "We love one another, but it's difficult living together."

She went on to describe her own intense preparation for a professional singing career and her deep immersion in the arts, a troubling contrast to Kent's complete lack of interest in attending any concert or performance—"even the ones where I'm performing."

Kent looked embarrassed. "I've made the effort to attend some of her long-haired affairs," he said, "and, honestly, it just feels like a big waste of time and money. I know nothing about music—except that Eleanor has her whole life wrapped up in it."

"He's just as committed to his research as I am to my music," Eleanor said. She explained that he was a successful biochemist in a large research company. "Kent has only two interests—chemical research and politics. You should see how he lights up when someone is willing to discuss politics with him. Which I'm *not*."

Kent admitted that he considers himself "basically tone deaf," lacking the capacity to *be* and *do* the things Eleanor needed from him. He felt she was unhappy with *who he basically is*—a guy who'd rather attend a political rally or something else "meaningful" than be bored stiff at some concert.

Eleanor had been told many times what a "handsome couple" they were, and this made her "try harder to make it work." Despite her best efforts, their connection was that of "a round peg in a square hole." In his company, she often felt unappreciated or simply invisible. His passion for what he did and what he believed always took precedence. Feeling like "an afterthought in his life," she craved a relationship in which she was valued for herself and her talent.

I first requested that Kent and Eleanor analyze the *Love, Liking and Lust Tool (#2)* during a therapy session. It quickly became apparent that the *Liking* dynamic was their biggest challenge and was basically missing.

Next, I requested they take home *Tool #8*: *Compatibility Rating*, get their scores and bring them to our next session.

It was no surprise to either of them that their scores were in the minus range: Kent's was minus 12, and Eleanor's was minus 14.

A few tears were shed as both agreed that the "Generally Incompatible" category accurately described their relationship. They definitely had major problems appreciating and nurturing one another. Both felt "significant distance" between them and a lack of emotional connection.

Neither Eleanor nor Kent felt they should go forward with marriage, which would insure even more unhappiness.

They worked out a rational and highly practical plan to "decompose" their relationship. Kent would move out of their "beautifully decorated condo," since he had wanted to "move closer to work, anyhow." Eleanor felt she could easily find a female roommate to share the rent.

The spirit of their parting was sad, but the decision was inevitable. They readily agreed to "remain friends and be helpful to each other" whenever they could.

POTENTIAL DISCRIMINATION

In a distinctly different case, I was counseling a racially mixed couple. Howard was 42, the highly extroverted owner of a successful local restaurant. His wife, Kerry, 39, was a sweet, diminutive secretary for a large developer. Married for six years, they were debating the issue of having a "racially mixed child."

Howard was concerned over "potential discrimination" if they were to have a child. He described himself as "black—that's African black-black. Kerry is soooo white-white that she can't even take much sun." He often teased her about her "lack of pigment."

Seeing how easily they laughed and joked together, it was obvious that they loved one another. Kerry was the one who initiated the idea of coming to see me for counseling over their "increasingly insurmountable dilemma." Should they risk having a racially mixed child?

Howard was less and less in favor of it, fearing their child might face "discrimination from both sides." Although his parents loved and accepted Kerry, they felt he "should have married a nice black lady." Her parents were less accepting of Howard, but had been willing to include him as "family," so long as the couple had no children.

But Kerry's heart had been set on having children—at least two or three. She was now "pushing Howard" toward getting her pregnant. At 39, she felt time running out on her biological clock.

Both of them were concerned about becoming "less compatible" because of this issue.

I had them take the "Compatibility Rating (*Tool #8*), and both scored in the "highly compatible" range with ratings of 19 and 20.

"See, I told you so," Kerry said. "There's nothing wrong with our marriage, dear Howard."

He responded that he couldn't agree more. They were deeply happy together, and he wanted to *keep* things that way. He saw no need to rock the boat with big changes.

"Yeah, *but…*" Kerry reiterated how much she wanted a family with Howard, how "sick and tired" she was of "kowtowing" to the prejudices of their parents. Their life should be up to *them*, not their parents.

Howard seemed conflicted in his own reasoning. On the one hand, he also longed to have a family with Kerry and felt strongly that they had the right to make their own decisions. On the other hand, he feared the reactions of a "significant percentage of folks who still cannot accept racially mixed couples." Both his parents and hers were firmly established in this category. Given this situation, what might a child of theirs suffer?

Although Howard was not put off by the parental reactions and prejudices, he was clearly apprehensive about society's norms and the possible conflicts their child might encounter. Our culture, he felt, "still contains many pockets of racism and discrimination."

Was it even *fair* to bring a racially mixed child into this world?

Kerry's answer was consistently, "Yes, it's our *family*."

Following many discussions and much open dialogue, Howard finally softened his stance. He agreed to simply stop using contraceptives for one year. There would be "no artificial anything"—just the purposeful omission of contraception. Kerry agreed to this.

They were happy and at peace with the issue as we ended the therapy. I'm not positive, but I believe Kerry did become pregnant during the second year, as she sent me a note saying, "We finally succeeded . . . I'm now pregnant, at 41."

As far as I know, they continued their "highly compatible" marriage and often reminded each other of their high scores.

NOTE:

The most accurate and effective use of *Tool #8*, Compatibility Rating, requires each partner to take the 50-statement survey privately, without discussing the items with anyone else. It's important to mark only the numbers that are essentially true for you, personally—including all positive and all negative statements. Then, follow the Directions.

▣ TOOL #8

COMPATIBILITY RATING:
How Compatible Are You?

DIRECTIONS: Please mark only the numbers that you believe are fundamentally true for you in your relationship. Do this privately, without consulting anyone else. Do not mark items that are only "half true" or of which you are unsure.

PERSON A _Taylor_
     (name)

  1. We do not share a clear vision of our future.

X **2.** I feel loved by my partner.

  3. My partner does not really understand me.

X **4.** My partner enjoys being in my company.

  5. I often feel lonely when I'm with my partner.

X **6.** I honestly listen to my partner's feelings and perceptions.

  7. I do not receive many compliments from my partner.

_X_ **8.** I feel sincerely appreciated by my partner.

___ **9.** My partner and I have trouble being affectionate.

_X_ **10.** We easily share decision making as a couple.

_X_ **11.** I do not completely trust my partner.

_X_ **12.** I can count on my partner to give me sincere encouragement.

___ **13.** I often feel embarrassed in social situations by my partner.

_X_ **14.** My partner stands up for me in public.

___ **15.** My partner often criticizes my actions.

_X_ **16.** We are definitely proud of each other.

___ **17.** I feel my partner doesn't really like me.

_X_ **18.** I am the most important person in my partner's life.

___ **19.** I hesitate to share intimate thoughts with my partner.

_X_ **20.** We laugh easily and frequently together.

___ **21.** I often feel picked on or put down by my partner.

_X_ **22.** My partner is open to my ideas and opinions in most situations.

___ **23.** We seldom feel joyful when we are together.

_X_ **24.** Sex is a satisfactory part of our relationship.

___ **25.** I am seldom the top priority in my partner's life.

_X_ **26.** My partner gives me meaningful and thoughtful feedback.

___ **27.** We both experience feelings of on-going resentment.

_X_ **28.** As a couple, we look forward to sensual moments and touching each other.

___ **29.** My partner lacks a need for closeness with me.

_X_ **30.** I feel safe expressing my emotions with my partner.

___ **31.** We seldom resolve disagreements between us.

next page

X 32. My partner seldom takes me for granted.

___ 33. My partner does not protect me emotionally in social situations.

X 34. I respect my partner for who she/he is.

___ 35. We have trouble with jealousy in our relationship.

X 36. My partner respects my wishes and views.

___ 37. We both lack the feeling of being cherished.

X 38. I am grateful to have my partner in my life.

___ 39. I find it difficult to praise my partner.

X 40. My partner really knows how to treat me right.

___ 41. I feel a lack of compassion from my partner.

X 42. We work well together on projects.

___ 43. I often feel neglected or overlooked by my partner.

X 44. We provide a "safe haven" for the other within our relationship.

___ 45. My partner often feels unappreciated by me.

X 46. We really enjoy spending time alone as a couple.

___ 47. We do not treat each other as allies and best friends.

X 48. Under stress, we remain open to the ideas and feelings of the other.

___ 49. Often we feel shut-down or hurt by each other.

X 50. The trust between us is basically unshakable.

172

SCORING THE COMPATIBILITY RATING:
PERSON A

2. 1. Count the total of **EVEN** numbered items you have selected to get your *Plus Score.*

1. 2. Count the total of **ODD** numbered items you have selected to get your *Minus Score.*

___ 3. Subtract the Minus Score from the Plus Score to determine the DIFFERENCE.
(**Note:** The DIFFERENCE may be a positive or negative number.) *24*

___ 4. Find your **Compatibility Rating** in one of the following categories. Record your Rating on this page.

PERSONAL NOTES PAGE:

Record your indivdual thoughts, reactions, comments, and questions below.

DIRECTIONS: Please mark only the numbers that you believe are fundamentally *true* **for you** in your relationship. Do this *privately*, without consulting anyone else. Do **not** mark items that are only "half true" or of which you are unsure.

PERSON B _____
(name)

__ **1.** We do not share a clear vision of our future.

__ **2.** I feel loved by my partner.

__ **3.** My partner does not really understand me.

__ **4.** My partner enjoys being in my company.

__ **5.** I often feel lonely when I'm with my partner.

__ **6.** I honestly listen to my partner's feelings and perceptions.

__ **7.** I do not receive many compliments from my partner.

__ **8.** I feel sincerely appreciated by my partner.

__ **9.** My partner and I have trouble being affectionate.

__ **10.** We easily share decision making as a couple.

__ **11.** I do not completely trust my partner.

_X_ **12.** I can count on my partner to give me sincere encouragement.

___ **13.** I often feel embarrassed in social situations by my partner.

_X_ **14.** My partner stands up for me in public.

_X_ **15.** My partner often criticizes my actions.

_X_ **16.** We are definitely proud of each other.

___ **17.** I feel my partner doesn't really like me.

_X_ **18.** I am the most important person in my partner's life.

___ **19.** I hesitate to share intimate thoughts with my partner.

_X_ **20.** We laugh easily and frequently together.

___ **21.** I often feel picked on or put down by my partner.

_X_ **22.** My partner is open to my ideas and opinions in most situations.

___ **23.** We seldom feel joyful when we are together.

_X_ **24.** Sex is a satisfactory part of our relationship.

___ **25.** I am seldom the top priority in my partner's life.

_X_ **26.** My partner gives me meaningful and thoughtful feedback.

___ **27.** We both experience feelings of on-going resentment.

_X_ **28.** As a couple, we look forward to sensual moments and touching each other.

___ **29.** My partner lacks a need for closeness with me.

_X_ **30.** I feel safe expressing my emotions with my partner.

___ **31.** We seldom resolve disagreements between us.

next page

_X_ **32.** My partner seldom takes me for granted.

___ **33.** My partner does not protect me emotionally in social situations.

_X_ **34.** I respect my partner for who she/he is.

___ **35.** We have trouble with jealousy in our relationship.

_X_ **36.** My partner respects my wishes and views.

___ **37.** We both lack the feeling of being cherished.

_X_ **38.** I am grateful to have my partner in my life.

___ **39.** I find it difficult to praise my partner.

_X_ **40.** My partner really knows how to treat me right.

___ **41.** I feel a lack of compassion from my partner.

___ **42.** We work well together on projects.

___ **43.** I often feel neglected or overlooked by my partner.

_X_ **44.** We provide a "safe haven" for the other within our relationship.

___ **45.** My partner often feels unappreciated by me.

_X_ **46.** We really enjoy spending time alone as a couple.

___ **47.** We do not treat each other as allies and best friends.

_X_ **48.** Under stress, we remain open to the ideas and feelings of the other.

___ **49.** Often we feel shut-down or hurt by each other.

_X_ **50.** The trust between us is basically unshakable.

SCORING THE COMPATIBILITY RATING:
PERSON B

24 1. Count the total of **EVEN** numbered items you have selected
to get your *Plus Score.*

1 2. Count the total of **ODD** numbered items you have selected
to get your *Minus Score.*

— 3. Subtract the Minus Score from the Plus Score to determine
the DIFFERENCE.
(**Note:** The DIFFERENCE may be a positive or negative
number.) *23*

— 4. Find your **Compatibility Rating** in one of the following
categories. Record your Rating on this page.

PERSONAL NOTES PAGE:

Record your indivdual thoughts, reactions, comments, and questions below.

COMPATIBILITY RATING SCALE

T-24 R-23

1) **Highly Compatible** **+17 to 25**
(Much in common; a "natural fit;" comfortable together,
communication is easy.)

2) **Generally Compatible** **+11 to 16**
(Overall, a good relationship with support and trust,
along with some problems.)

3) **Slightly Compatible** **+5 to 10**
(Getting along with some serious differences to work on.)

4) **Neutral with severe problems** **+4 to −4**
(The negative aspects are equal to the positive,
many serious differences to resolve.)

5) **Slightly Incompatible** **−5 to −10**
(Problems outweigh the joy and benefit of being in the
relationship, lack of respect for differences.)

6) **Generally Incompatible** **−11 to −16**
(Major problems appreciating and nurturing each other;
great distance and lack of connection.)

7) **Highly Incompatible** **−17 to −25**
(Severe hostility, anger with inability to empathize or solve
problems; emotionally stuck.)

DIRECTIONS FOR PERSONS A AND B:

1) Compare your "compatibility ratings"—and discuss the overall experience.

2) Arrange a 30-minute "date" (a mutually acceptable half-hour) to sit down with your partner to thoroughly discuss these items. You will both discuss why you marked, or did not mark sentence #1, then sentence #2, etc. in sequence.

3) Never allow your discussion time to go over 30 minutes in one day; put your ratings aside and arrange your next half-hour "date" at the end of each discussion.
You will most likely only discuss 6 to 8 items per "date."

9

RESOLVING CONFLICT:
"Turning Right"

"Life is difficult." These are the first three words in M. Scott Peck's classic book *The Road Less Traveled*. I can still recall the impact of this sentence and the many lessons that were to follow. Yes, life is full of difficulties, problems and conflicts, many of which feel as though they can never be resolved.

All of us have suffered from conflict in our love relationships. No one has escaped unscathed. Yet we all "go back for more," since at some level *we all desire to love and be loved.*
The fact that we all suffer conflict in our love relationships is not the point. Rather, it is how we *choose* (either consciously or unconsciously) *to handle the conflict* that matters.

In order to successfully navigate the waters of conflict, we need *self-discipline.* We need the *Tools* and the personal determination to face our problems and the emotional pain involved in their resolution. Far more courage is required to face our conflicts directly than to avoid them.

If we can muster the will to create an *open heart* and an *open mind*, the chances for resolving almost any conflict or problem are excellent. If, on the other hand, we shut off our feelings with a *closed heart* and *mind*, resolution mostly becomes impossible.

However, when conflict is addressed directly, the probability for experiencing pain and fear is high. It's "no picnic" to delve objectively into our problems.

FULL DISCLOSURE

I'm reminded of a pleasant couple, ages 32 and 34, with one little girl, age 4, in which the husband could not bear to face the truth about his family history.

Sherry adored her husband, Doug, and respected his "business acumen." Doug had worked hard to build his small furniture business—part retail, part wholesale.

He inherited "parts of the business" and a few assets from his father. Although married for six years, Sherry never "had the pleasure of meeting Doug's dad." She had the impression that he "had moved to Europe following the sudden death of Doug's mom."

Doug admitted he'd never felt comfortable discussing his parents with anyone. He acknowledged that he'd tried to "forget all about it." The whole story about his parents and his growing up seemed shrouded in mystery.

In the end, through many tears and much grief, it became clear why Doug had become so neurotic—compulsive over money, taxes, savings, the IRS, budgets, etc.

Sherry said, "Our *one* big problem seems to be the control of money. I respect Doug's ability to keep that furniture company up and running. At the same time, he's taken away any freedom that I might have to buy groceries, clothes, things for our little girl. Every last penny must be accounted for, as part of Doug's budget.

Now 34, Sherry had been a successful dental hygienist prior to the birth of their daughter and was "used to" making her own money. Over the last four-plus years, with her not working, Doug's purse strings had been pulled ever tighter.

"It's not that I need a lot of money, but I do need a little freedom to run the household," Sherry said. "What's wrong with Doug?" The three of us agreed to explore the real reasons behind his apparent need for complete control.

Doug's compulsive "money management," as he called it, was certainly related to his parental history. His mother had been an alcoholic and drug user most of his life. His father, always sober, "struggled mightily to earn enough money from the business to cover all the bills she was responsible for. Doug was 22 when she died of an overdose.

"My dad loved her and was devastated by her death; he was also broke and unable to pay all the bills Mom had created. He felt like a failure—a literal prisoner of the debt she left him with."

The worst part was that Doug's dad had been found "guilty of income tax fraud" five years before his mother's death and "served three months in jail."

Doug was 17 at the time and "barely made it through high school," taking on small, menial jobs and helping out at the furniture store, where "the manager managed to keep the doors open until Dad got out." Doug felt humiliated over the whole situation. The year after his mother's death, Doug's dad was so depressed, so demoralized, that Doug persuaded him to "start over"—move to England, where he had two close cousins, get a job in manufacturing (or whatever) and meet new people.

Finally, his dad agreed. Since Doug was an only child, it was simple for his dad to sign over the furniture company to him. At age 23, Doug became the owner of a small struggling business. "What a mess it all was."

Doug was glad to see his dad "make a clean break and start over in London." He blamed his mother's addictions for everything; even his dad's "income tax fraud was an attempt to cover Mom's many bills."

"It makes me so angry, so fearful that I might ever fall into the same trap," Doug said. "I *don't* ever want to be like *either of my parents*. I want to just play by the book." And so he developed his compulsively tight grip on all money matters.

After weeks of explanation, exploration and filling in the blanks, Sherry gained a clear understanding of her husband. "Now I understand why I've never met his dad and why Doug has developed this money issue."

Doug was incredibly relieved once Sherry understood the whole picture. He explained that she had never accumulated a penny of credit card debt and was extremely smart about her shopping and expenses. "I trust my wife completely," he said. "That's why I married her."

"Then why," she asked quietly, "don't you trust me to share the burden of our budget? I'm very good at that stuff!"

It slowly dawned on Doug that he had taken away all control and decision-making from his wife—and "for no good reason." His heart and mind were now open, exploratory and inclusive.

Sherry was getting ready to go back to work as a dental hygienist when Doug suggested that she first try "coming on board with me at the store." He realized how difficult he had made the money management for both of them.

"I'm more free now, Sherry, to share this whole mess with you. I've been such an ass, trying to control every penny."

Having gained enormous insight into himself, Doug now understood that he no longer had to *prove* to himself that he wasn't like either of his parents.

Sherry agreed to try her hand at "accounting and some sales" at the store. As it turned out, she was a "natural with the accounting" and took a short class in marketing to help boost sales.

I continued to see them periodically for "check-up sessions." Within six months Sherry proved she had real marketing talent. She expanded the customer base and got the business "on the Internet . . . for custom orders." Her work alone "doubled the gross income of the business."

Doug was ecstatically happy and always gave Sherry full credit for this turn-around, thanking her profusely. He reported how free he now felt, "sharing it all" at home and in the business. It was easy now to remember why he had fallen deeply in love and wanted to marry her—she was "nothing like my mom." He truly loved her and eventually opened his heart so that he could "encourage her to be all she can be!"

"It's wonderful to have a real co-pilot," Doug said. "I can't believe I let my fears control all of our business and every last penny of our income." He counted himself "incredibly fortunate" to have such a smart and talented wife.

Tool #9, "Resolving Conflict," was a major help to Doug and Sherry; "turning right" and discussing their fears became natural for them both.

ALL GROWN UP

I recall another case in which conflict was painfully present on two different fronts: between the two partners and also between them and her parents.

Gwen was 18, and Shawn had "just turned 28." She was highly

extroverted, dramatic, headstrong, rebellious and extremely good looking. She tried to appear much older by wearing lots of makeup and jewelry. She continually reminded me that she would "soon be 19—in a couple of months."

Shawn was suave, smooth, overly polite, handsome and seductive in a narcissistic way. He had been a "clothes model" for a short time and now worked in an elite men's clothing store. He had "never bothered much with college," since he felt sure he would soon land a part in a movie. His ultimate goal was to become a "supreme actor."

Gwen and Shawn had fallen in love, and Gwen insisted that they "wanted to get married as soon as possible." This situation had snowballed into a major conflict. Gwen wanted to *elope immediately,* go to Las Vegas and get married this week. Shawn felt they should "wait until we save some money." He couldn't see Gwen being happy in his "shabby apartment." Nor was he "technically ready" for a lifelong marriage commitment this week.

Gwen was "ready for it all—yesterday!" She was "grown up" and longed for a home of her own. She believed that "the money will come, if Shawn works hard enough."

Gwen's parents were aghast and sent the two of them to me for counseling. (Her parents had been my marriage counseling clients years earlier.) They were a stable, steadfast couple determined to raise a healthy family. They had two boys, both younger teenagers (14 and 16) and Gwen (18). She behaved like a "firecracker—always going off and making a big show." And now Shawn was an important part of that show—a situation they were less than happy about.

Gwen's parents were willing to pay for all counseling sessions, either with Gwen alone or including Shawn. They were seriously concerned that Gwen "would use sex, etc." to convince Shawn they should "go to Vegas and get married," a prospect that left her parents feeling panicky.

Although Gwen was the oldest of their three children, they felt both boys had "better heads on their shoulders" than she did—and made better decisions.

I counseled Gwen, both alone and together with Shawn. It became increasingly clear that he had no real intention of getting married, at least not in this decade.

When confronted with finances and the prospect of supporting a wife, he seemed to crumble under the burden and started making pointed references to his ex-girlfriend (to intentionally alienate Gwen, in my opinion).

Gwen became irate and extremely jealous. Wasn't she beautiful enough? What did Shawn see in this "phony clothes model?" Didn't he *love her* enough to get married?

Shawn hung his head and finally admitted that he was "not marriage material . . . Gwen deserves more than this." And yes, he had "seen" his ex-girlfriend . . . "only twice."

Gwen was shattered. She became hateful and defensive, screamed and yelled at Shawn and told him to "get out" of my office. Shawn left slowly and silently—and I think gladly. She never heard from him again.

For a short time, Gwen tried to blame her parents for "breaking us up" and "ruining our engagement." Although I showed empathy for her broken heart, I consistently talked with her about how *assuming responsibility* for all of her own actions and reactions was an essential ingredient for maturity.

It was difficult for Gwen to grasp this concept, but with months of confrontative psychotherapy it gradually sank in. How could her parents have broken them up, when they were the ones who insisted on financing all this therapy to help the couple?

How could Gwen assume that Shawn also wanted marriage immediately, as she did, when he was *never* the one who mentioned marriage? Nor had he ever asked Gwen to marry him. I pointed out how concerned Shawn was over his "low income" and inability to rent "even a small house." Also, his dream was to land an acting job in Hollywood—not support a wife and purchase a home!

As Gwen accepted more responsibility for her actions and feelings, I was able gradually to show her how everything she did was *her decision.* She argued about most topics, until she "saw the light."

"Love, or being in love," she insisted, was "a *feeling.*"

Yes, I agreed, but how a person *acts* on those feelings is still a decision. Whether consciously or unconsciously, when anyone acts physically or mentally on a feeling, that is a personal decision . . . a *choice.*

I went on to explain that *real power* meant that a person became *conscious* of her decisions (i.e., her choices) and took personal *responsibility* for them. Gwen was curious about "real power" and grew significantly from exploring these concepts.

The use of *Tool #9: "Resolving Conflict"* was a rough passage for Gwen, but eventually she made the *decision* to "turn right"— that is, to keep an open heart and an open mind, with no defensiveness. I kept explaining *Tool #9* and demonstrating how "turning right" would give her more power, more freedom, and more genuine love (from everyone—her parents, her brothers, her future dates and romantic partners).

THE VALUE OF "TURNING RIGHT"

This *Tool #9: "Resolving Conflict,"* and my concept of "turning right' have been helpful for many people in many different circumstances. Having an open heart and an open mind is *always preferable* to being closed—even in the face of hostility, rage, disappointment and grief.

The following chart, which is *Tool #9*, is intended as a guide, a map for increasing awareness and decision-making. In many cases, this "map" can be helpful as you consider the consequences of "turning right" or "turning left."

Both you, as an individual, and your partner have the personal responsibility of making these decisions on a daily basis.

I've had the privilege of witnessing how numerous fights, misunderstandings, and potential breakdowns in communication have been avoided completely by the two people simply becoming *conscious* and "turning right."

In fact, for many couples, especially those who are less verbal than others, this simple injunction to "turn right" has become a substitute *"code" phrase* for what they might have previously said in anger. These two words—*"turn right"*—are far less inflammatory and can help the partner become more *conscious of their choices.*

The specific meaning of "turn right" can refer to anything from " Think about what you're doing" to "Don't get defensive" to "Open your heart" to "Don't be an ass" to "Take responsibility for your own actions." When your partner exclaims, "Turn right!" you generally know what they mean.

Enjoy the journey!

☑ TOOL #9

RESOLVING CONFLICT:
"Turning Right"

DIRECTIONS:

1) Take time to study the following flow chart; see how one decision can lead to many other consequences.

2) With the choice of initially "turning right" or "turning left" there are numerous results— either wanted or unwanted.

3) By raising our *consciousness* and having the *self-discipline* to make positive decisions (i.e., turn right)— we can save ourselves much grief and unwanted consequences.

4) Discuss with your partner how:

   A) Each of you can make more *conscious* decisions.

   B) How you might get the *spirit* of your whole relationship to "turn right."

   C) How you might want to use the code words—of "turn right"—to help you, as a couple, *avoid* misunderstandings, hurt feelings and other problems.

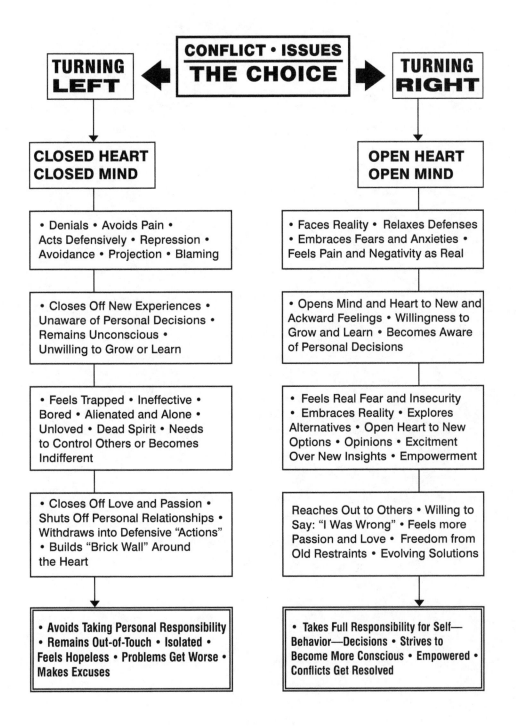

CONFLICT • ISSUES
THE CHOICE

TURNING LEFT ◀   ▶ TURNING RIGHT

CLOSED HEART CLOSED MIND

OPEN HEART OPEN MIND

• Denials • Avoids Pain •
Acts Defensively • Repression •
Avoidance • Projection • Blaming

• Faces Reality • Relaxes Defenses
• Embraces Fears and Anxieties •
Feels Pain and Negativity as Real

• Closes Off New Experiences •
Unaware of Personal Decisions •
Remains Unconscious •
Unwilling to Grow or Learn

• Opens Mind and Heart to New and
Ackward Feelings • Willingness to
Grow and Learn • Becomes Aware
of Personal Decisions

• Feels Trapped • Ineffective •
Bored • Alienated and Alone •
Unloved • Dead Spirit • Needs
to Control Others or Becomes
Indifferent

• Feels Real Fear and Insecurity
• Embraces Reality • Explores
Alternatives • Open Heart to New
Options • Opinions • Excitment
Over New Insights • Empowerment

• Closes Off Love and Passion •
Shuts Off Personal Relationships •
Withdraws into Defensive "Actions"
• Builds "Brick Wall" Around
the Heart

Reaches Out to Others • Willing to
Say: "I Was Wrong" • Feels more
Passion and Love • Freedom from
Old Restraints • Evolving Solutions

• Avoids Taking Personal Responsibility
• Remains Out-of-Touch • Isolated •
Feels Hopeless • Problems Get Worse •
Makes Excuses

• Takes Full Responsibility for Self—
Behavior—Decisions • Strives to
Become More Conscious • Empowered •
Conflicts Get Resolved

10

ATTITUDE AND MINDSET:
Finding a Different Street

As our final *Tool* I've chosen the simplest and potentially the most profound of all the *Tools*. It can involve the least amount of time from you—or possibly the most.

There are many times in any individual's life when we fall into a problem simply from the *force of habit*. Our consciousness may be at a low point; or our mindfulness may have drifted elsewhere. Given the stresses of modern life, it's difficult to assume responsibility for all our actions every minute of the day. Consequently, we tend to remain stuck in whatever issue has become our habitual focus of attention.

Seeing ourselves accurately becomes problematic, and comprehending our role in the creation of our own dilemmas all but impossible.

Thus we continue to make the *same mistakes* over and over, as if we were blindfolded. The blinders do offer a kind of comfort, helping us remain in denial about having any responsibility for the circumstances we continually struggle with.

At some point, many of us experience a shock-point that may steer us toward a real *turning point*. As our consciousness expands, we begin to see ourselves differently.

Most significantly, we start to see our own role in the creation of our problems and begin taking appropriate responsibility for our choices. Most of us still make many of the same mistakes, but we have a glimmer of new awareness, a new awkwardness with our old habits and a sense of impending fresh possibilities.

As we begin making different choices and decisions, we're more awake and aware of retreating from our old patterns. Though it's still tempting to fall back into those familiar habits, we feel increasingly empowered to explore better alternatives.

We're able to perceive our choices and consider various *options* with greater clarity. At this point we actually feel conscious enough to choose a different program or pathway. And so we do.

It feels good to realize that a *different mindset*, a different physical program, a different value system—even a completely new paradigm—are well within our reach.

The more choices we make in this new paradigm, the more comfortable we feel with the "new normal" that we've established.

Portia Nelson's eloquent poem "Autobiography in Five Chapters" (on page 199) provides a compelling metaphor for the journey from the unexamined life (crammed with habits, familiar thought patterns and routines) to the consciously lived (mindful) life.

CHANGING VIEWS: A Different Street

Years ago I worked with a charming young engaged couple whom I'll call Karen and Ken. Obviously deeply in love and devoted to each other, they shared a common cultural background (family values, Catholic religion, liberal politics, etc.) and had amazingly compatible "lovemaps" describing their ideal mate.

They seemed seriously stuck in the inherited moral dictates and religious values of their parents—so much so that they never thought about how vital it was for them to address the issue that was now troubling them and the reason for their coming to see me: namely, their views about *abortion*.

Karen was two months pregnant, and both agreed that this condition was unwanted. Both were noticeably uncomfortable even discussing this issue with me. They had no doubt as to what position their priest would take. Twenty-three and twenty-four years old, both had recently graduated from college and were seeking higher-paying jobs. They wanted to marry as soon as their financial situation would allow.

The same week they first visited my office I had run across Nelson's powerful poem. Could this poem, I wondered, perhaps help Karen and Ken? Could it offer them a pathway through their dilemma other than the only option their religion was able to provide?

I had the poem printed out, gave each of them a copy, and asked them to study and discuss the meaning in relation to their situation. Knowing how spiritually oriented Ken and Karen were, I felt this poem might impact their discussion and decision-making.

In our session the following week, they both expressed excitement over a *"new-found freedom"* they were considering—the liberty to determine their own religious path, guided by their own moral parameters. Although both expressed great respect for their parents' values, the Catholic Church and their upbringing, they now believed they had the "right" and the "freedom" to set their own course. They alone could make the decisions necessary to bring about their own "highest good" and future wellbeing.

They both felt that abortion was "the only rational . . . the only acceptable choice" they had. There was no way they could afford to raise a child at this time. They had to take some painful steps. Resolution of their excruciating dilemma followed quickly as they agreed to *"walk down a different street."*

WALKING DOWN A DIFFERENT STREET TOGETHER

I remember another couple's hateful philosophical debate over the "death penalty." The wife, Debbie, was vociferously opposed to any form of "killing," based on her strict religious upbringing. Her husband, Paul, was a "rational, non-religious type" who felt equally passionate about "the horrible, irrational expense of keeping all these convicted killers alive, well fed and protected in jail, at the taxpayers' expense."

Debbie would reply vehemently that it still wasn't right "for the State to kill anyone."

Both had fierce feelings about the issue, refused to "turn right" *(Tool #9),* and were uninterested in *Tool #10*: ATTITUDE AND MINDSET: *Finding a Different Street.*

I explained in some detail why Debbie and Paul were initially so attracted to one another (i.e., their highly compatible lovemaps, reflecting their mutual deep passion and caring about doing the "right thing"). Both were willing to "take a stand" for what they believed, in addition to having much more in common than most couples.

Eventually, I had them practice *"reverse role playing,"* where Debbie would assume Paul's perspective and he would assume hers. This process was interesting and emotional for them, and it was exciting for me to see them both softening.

Finally, Paul, seeing Debbie in tears, said, "I think we just *'turned right.'*" Their *hearts and minds opened*, and they were suddenly ready to consider the poem that is the vital core of *Tool #10*. As they studied it, in one session they were able to "walk down a different street" together—with much greater empathy and compassion for their partner.

▣ TOOL #10

ATTITUDE AND MINDSET:
Finding a Different Street

In order to derive the most benefit from this exercise it is important to:

1) Study the meaning of Portia Nelson's poem, "Autobiography in Five Chapters" on the following page.

2) Ask yourself *How* and *If* this metaphor applies to any aspect of your life and/or your relationship.

3) What would *"walking down a different street"* mean in terms of your *decisions*— your daily life—perhaps the *changes* that you desire to make?

Autobiography in Five Chapters

1) I walk down the street.
    There is a deep hole in the sidewalk.
    I fall in.
    I am lost . . . I am hopeless.
    It isn't my fault.
    It takes forever to find a way out.

2) I walk down the same street.
    There is a deep hole in the sidewalk.
    I pretend I don't see it.
    I fall in again.
    I can't believe I'm in the same place.
    But it isn't my fault.
    It still takes a long time to get out.

3) I walk down the same street.
    There is a deep hole in the sidewalk.
    I see it is there.
    I still fall in . . . it's a habit
    My eyes are open.
    I know where I am.
    It is my fault.
    I get out immediately.

4) I walk down the same street.
    There is a deep hole in the sidewalk.
    I walk around it.

5) I walk down a different street.

—*Portia Nelson*

INSTRUCTIONS FOR TOOL #10:

ATTITUDE AND MINDSET: Finding a Different Street

1. The concept of *change* is central here. Do we truly want to be awakened? Is it worth what it costs, seeing reality more accurately? To grow, even when it might be painful or inconvenient?

2. When we make the choice *not* to fall back into our habitual blind spots and keep repeating our old mistakes, the feeling of clarity and freedom can be liberating.
This world of new possibilities may feel awkward at first, but as we practice our new habits they become increasingly comfortable. The "different street" looks more and more like home base.

3. Please spend as much time as you need contemplating this rich and simple poem. For some individuals and couples it has provided a powerful awakening and significant change. *Reflect* on the central metaphor in Nelson's poem and consider how it may *apply to your own life situation*—especially to your love relationship.

* * *

NOTE:
Some of the previous *Tools* may have been more (or less) helpful in your unique situation. I hope you'll go back and give each of them a fair chance to become your friend, if you haven't already. Let's give love a fair chance to thrive.

— PART III —

IF YOU NEED FURTHER HELP

I hope that at least one—maybe even several—of these *10 Tools* have been especially meaningful for you and/or your partner. That is my goal in making the *Tools* available.

Looking back over my four decades of clinical practice, I've sometimes felt distressed that a significant number of my former clients had *not* been helped by their previous therapists, despite months—and sometimes *years*— of costly therapy.

In some cases, it appeared that their therapy experience was a waste of their time and money, though they suffered no emotional harm in the process. Still, there were no gains in their decision-making, self-esteem or life circumstances. Often, their presenting problem had not even been addressed, let alone *solved*.

In a smaller number of cases, actual *damage* had been done to the individual (or couple), depending on their values and living situation. In a few cases, the carnage created by the therapist's ego, rigidity and/or projection of their ideals and values onto their client(s) created a horrible dilemma. This was disheartening for me to uncover.

In one case, for example, I clearly remember a young Asian couple who were shattered by their experience in therapy. They were highly compatible, deeply in love and came to see me because the wife was experiencing a sexual issue (i.e., vaginismus—resulting from a date-rape trauma years before).

This couple had been living in a large house with the husband's parents as well as his grandmother, his sister, her husband and the couple's 4-year-old son. (This was a common arrangement for immigrant families, designed to economize on rent.)

The therapist had apparently judged this housing situation to be totally unacceptable; he urged the young husband to "grow up," get a better job (i.e., earn more money) and get a home of their own. Thus, this *therapist totally missed* the basic reason this couple had sought counseling to begin with!

This ill-advised "counsel" threw the husband into depression and self-doubt. The wife felt more traumatized and frustrated then ever. The therapist had *projected his own values* and opinions onto the couple—which is *never appropriate* in professional therapy. The results were extremely unfortunate.

I had to explain this horrendous error on the therapist's part—and create a *solid* program for the true healing of this young wife's trauma (i.e., vaginismus).

THE NEED FOR EFFECTIVE THERAPY

Most of us have little or no preparation for—or experience in—seeking out an effective therapist. This usually isn't an issue we think of discussing with close friends, co-workers, or even relatives.

Nor would most of us know how to end a therapy arrangement in which we're not being empowered or guided toward helpful options and solutions. In such situations a client needs enough self-esteem and sense of entitlement to put an end to useless (or damaging) sessions.

Of course, it's better to choose a healthy, effective therapist right at the start. In cases where the *Tools* are not sufficient—and in-person professional therapy is needed—it's important to consider the following characteristics. A good therapist will certainly possess some—and ideally all—of the following traits:

1. Empathy and Compassion

The ability to put oneself in the shoes of the client is essential. To understand and experience his/her perspective on the central dilemma is vital—without projecting one's own feelings, values or judgments. We need and expect this kind of empathy from our deepest friendships, closest family members—especially—from our mate and certainly from a professional therapist.

In addition, the practice of steadfast compassion is even more vital for a successful therapist or marriage counselor. Compassion includes not only the warmth of emotion-based *empathy* but also the *objectivity* to make good judgments and the rational strength to make occasionally quick and helpful decisions.

Even when a client's complaints sound preposterous, it's essential that the therapist comprehend *how* and *why* certain problems evolved. This is necessary even when the situation is something the therapist would never have created or chosen for her/himself.

2. Intelligence and Discernment

This involves the ability to devise—or at least locate—appropriate solutions and various alternatives for the client to consider. It's the therapist's job to empower the client (or the couple) to think about different pathways for problem-solving, different methods of reasoning, logic and emotional evaluation.

The therapist must discern what is important and relevant for solving the immediate problem, especially when the client is clearly unable to make such choices. It is the therapist's responsibility to keep the session "on track."

3. Humility and Non-Judgmental Neutrality

It is important for a good therapist to be willing to be questioned, to be wrong, to see an alternative or better way. It is essential not to impose on the client one's own "program," values or opinions. I once had a professor in college who would chastise us (his students) for daring to question him. With that attitude, he could never have been an effective therapist—nor was he as effective a teacher as he could have been.

A framework of *non-judgment* surrounding the client and his/her problems is vital to a therapist's ability to probe deeply and get to the bottom of the person's issues. An attitude of neutrality and acceptance of the client (or couple) and their history, choices and extenuating circumstances is essential.

These subtle attitudes all contribute to the therapist's effectiveness in offering counsel and feedback that actually enable the client to make choices for her/his own highest good.

4. Presence and Focus

The ability to "be here now" is never out of date. The act of giving full attention to the client and what she/he is expressing or saying is at the core of effective therapy. Not being distracted by outside events or extraneous topics is vital; while it's necessary to let the client lead the conversation and choose his/her topics, it's likewise essential for the therapist to keep the focus on the presenting complaint(s).

The ability to stay "on course" and use the precious minutes of the therapy session to gain a deeper understanding of the client (or couple) is vital. The therapist must use this time to create the methods, options and *Tools* that will enable the client(s) to actually resolve problems or redefine a situation.

FINDING SOMEONE DIFFERENT

Although I hope that the *Tools* presented in this book will help many good relationships grow and mature, I also understand that actual counseling sessions are sometimes necessary.

In certain instances, it's simply *not* enough to "become your own therapist," as suggested in these pages. When actual counseling becomes a need, I urge you to at least consider the four areas I've outlined above as well as the Red Flags listed below. I trust these guidelines may assist you in finding the right therapist from the beginning.

RED FLAGS: WHAT TO AVOID

Sometimes it becomes necessary to change therapists—to fire the one you have—in order to avoid certain attitudes, limitations or prejudices. Or you may feel the therapist you're currently working with is simply not equipped to handle your unique problem(s) or circumstances.

In my opinion, it is not only your *right* but also your *responsibility* to seek out a therapist who will not hamper your growth and your objective decision-making or prejudice the outcome of your journey in therapy.

Therapists should avoid being caught up in certain side issues (e.g., social, cultural, political or religious beliefs) that serve only as distractions from the core issue. An effective therapist will consistently help the client (or couple) stay focused on the essential elements of their presenting problem. It is important to consistently counsel clients in ways that empower them to make choices that are genuinely useful and healthy. In my opinion, anything that fails to somehow empower the client would be considered a therapeutic failure.

It is always important for the therapist not to take up precious time digressing into her/his own perspective, opinions, history or personal examples that are not essentially helpful to the client.

Over my four decades of doing psychotherapy and marriage counseling, I have observed certain attitudes and belief systems among some therapists that I consider counter- productive—and occasionally dangerous—to the client and the actual process of therapy.

Here are some of my observations—about the attitudes, biases and prejudices that *limit a therapist's ability* to do objective counseling.

AVOID THERAPISTS WHO THINK THAT:

1)   Online affairs don't really count as affairs; it's only the computer and not a real person.

2)   It's "all in God's hands," and you have no objective control over the outcome of your decisions.

3)   Affairs and cheating are "natural" and sometimes acceptable, especially for men: "Boys will be boys."

4) Certain topics should be "off limits" in a therapy session (e.g., death, theft, incest, abortion, drugs, gay sex, having affairs).

5) If you technically didn't have intercourse—or if you didn't really care for the sex partner—then it's not really an "affair."

6) The psychological problems of the betrayed partner are the real cause of the mate's acting out (lying, cheating, abuse).

7) There are definite "time lines" or expiration dates for when you should be over a trauma or betrayal—put it aside and be done with it.

8) The therapist gets to decide if you're "over-reacting" and putting too much emphasis on a certain incident or topic.

9) Your childhood wounds are a thing of the past and need to be forgotten; move on.

10) All problems in a marriage "take two." If one partner has an affair or violates the trust of the other, both are equally responsible.

11) Gay sex, seduction and flirting do not count as "affairs" in a heterosexual relationship.

12) The rules of commitment and integrity do not apply under certain circumstances.

13) Lying, cheating and deception should automatically be forgiven, once the betrayer confesses.

14) It is impossible to make any progress in therapy until "all sins are forgiven" and we have a clean slate.

15) We need to extinguish anger and rage as soon as possible, because they are counterproductive and dysfunctional in therapy.

16) We should save the marriage at any cost—or "for the sake of the children" ("the business," "our finances," "the family's reputation," etc.)

17) Your own insecurities and fears are what cause your partner to treat you the way he/she does.

18) Private use of pornography that excludes your partner does not count as actual cheating.

There are many case examples in which each of the above attitudes or beliefs of a therapist has caused definite *harm to the client*.

You may need to directly question any prospective counselor or therapist about her/his assumptions. In my opinion, any one of the 18 beliefs/biases above would be sufficient reason to *call a halt* to any further sessions and *seek out a new therapist*.

If you feel intimidated about asking probing questions, consider this a signal that you need to push even harder for answers.

All human beings, including therapists, have some biases. Excellent therapists have been trained, however, *not to allow* their *personal fears, wounds, defense mechanisms* or *traumas* to affect their judgment or work as a professional.

Most therapists have undergone individual therapy as a client in order to resolve their personal issues and thus avoid inflicting them on clients.

MY BEST ADVICE FOR FINDING A THERAPIST

Don't be afraid to ask for referrals; get recommendations from friends, co-workers, professional organizations—wherever you can find them.

In most cases, you won't have the opportunity to assess these criteria until you've had at least one—and maybe several—sessions in person. As you experience these, if you're not comfortable or don't feel this is the right therapist for you as a couple, feel free to seek out another professional. It's your *time,* your *money,* and your *love relationship*—which may be one of the most precious assets you have—and worth protecting.

Do not continue with a therapist that you do not feel has your highest good in mind, or one who may lack the experience and methods necessary to help your unique situation. Do not continue therapy on a dead-end street; find someone different.

All these efforts—using some or all of the *Tools* and, if necessary, finding the right therapist—are designed to make the love you already have grow and thrive.

Whatever your path, I hope you succeed in making your intimate partnership the greatest treasure of your life.

BIBLIOGRAPHY

Baron-Cohen, Simon. *The Essential Difference: The Truth about the Male and Female Brain.* (Basic Books. New York. 2003).

Bloom, Linda and Charlie Bloom. *Happily Ever After and 39 Other Myths About Love.* (New World Library, Novato CA. 2016).

Bradberry, Travis and Jean Greaves. *Emotional Intelligence 2.0* (Talent Smart. San Diego CA. 2009).

Campbell, Susan and John Grey. *Five Minute Relationship Repair.* (New World Library. Novato CA. 2015).

Chapman, Gary. *The 5 Love Languages: The Secret to Love that Lasts.* (Northfield Publishing. Chicago IL. 2010).

Coldwell, Julia B. *The Relationship Skills Workbook.* (Sounds True. Boulder CO. 2014).

Goleman, Daniel. *Emotional Intelligence: Why It Can Matter More than I.Q.* (Bantam Books. New York. 1995).

Gottman, John and Joan De Claire. *The Relationship Cure.* (Random House. New York. 2001).

Gottman, John and Nan Silver. *The Seven Principles for Making Marriage Work.* (Random House. LLC/Harmony Books. New York. 2015).

Grey, John, Ph.D. *Men Are from Mars, Women Are from Venus: The Classic Guide to Understanding the Opposite Sex.* (New York. Harper Collins. 1992).

Hendrix, Harville. *Getting the Love You Want.* (Henry Holt & Co. New York. 1988).

Love, Patricia, Ed.D. and Steven Stosny, Ph.D. *How to Improve Your Marriage Without Talking about It: How to Save Your Marriage and Heal or Repair An Unhappy Relationship.* (New York. Broadway Books. 2007).

Nelson, Portia. *There's a Hole in My Sidewalk: The Romance of Self-Discovery.* (New York. Simon & Schuster. 1993).

Peck, M. Scott, M.D. *The Road Less Traveled.* (New York. Simon & Schuster. 1978).

Riso, Don Richard and Russ Hudson. *The Wisdom of the Enneagram.* New York. Bantam Books. 1999).

ABOUT THE AUTHOR

Mona Coates, Ph.D. is a psychotherapist and college professor emeritus of Sociology-Psychology/Human Sexuality. She is also a licensed marriage and family counselor, certified hypnotherapist, nationally certified sex therapist and sex educator. She has been in private practice since 1977.

She has produced several CD programs, conducted a wide range of seminars and professional workshops, directed two sex-education films and hosted her own cable television show, "Sexuality Today."

She is the primary author of the C-JES (Coates-Jacobs Enneagram Survey), *The Self-Scoring Book*, and *Sex, Love and Your Personality: The Nine Faces of Intimacy*.

CPSIA information can be obtained
at www.ICGtesting.com
Printed in the USA
LVHW01s0000180918
590504LV00010B/209/P